Y0-BND-106

MICROSOFT® EXCEL 2000
QUICK REFERENCE

Nancy Warner

201 West 103rd Street, Indianapolis, Indiana 46290

MICROSOFT® EXCEL 2000 QUICK REFERENCE

ISBN: 0-7897-2587-8

Library of Congress Catalog Card Number: 99-61235

Printed in the United States of America

First Printing: *March 2001*

03   02   01   4   3   2   1

TRADEMARKS

Publisher
Greg Wiegand

Acquisitions Editor
Stephanie McComb

Development Editor
Christy Parrish

Managing Editor
Thomas F. Hayes

Copy Editor
Molly Schaller

Indexer
Greg Pearson

Proofreader
Tricia Sterling

Technical Editor
Dave Bixler

Layout Technicians
Michael J. Poor
Louis Porter, Jr

Book Designer
Lousia Klucznik

ABOUT THE AUTHOR

Nancy Warner is a private consultant in the computer and publishing arenas currently focusing on freelance writing and development editing. She graduated from Purdue University in Computer Information Systems and has worked as an end user specialist and data access analyst. Along with the numerous computer books she has developed and edited, she has written or contributed to *Easy Office 2000*, *Easy Excel 2000*, *Microsoft Office 2000 Quick Reference*, *Microsoft Word 2000 Quick Reference*, *Special Edition Using Office 97*, *Platinum Edition Using Office 97*, *Easy Office 97, Second Edition*, *Teach Yourself Office 97 in 10 Minutes*, *Easy Windows NT Workstation 4.0*, and *How to Use Access 97*.

DEDICATION

I would like to dedicate this book to my friend Caroline. You are always ready to listen and make me laugh.

ACKNOWLEDGMENTS

I would like to thank Jim Minatel, Stephanie McComb, Angie Wethington, Greg Wiegand, Christy Parrish, and Dave Bixler for seeing these projects through.

INTRODUCTION

The Quick Reference series serves as a guide to look up information on specific software topics. This book contains an alphabetical listing of topics that will help you perform a desired task as quickly as possible. For example, if you want to know how to create an Excel table, you would reference "**T**" in the Excel section for **Table**.

ABOUT THIS BOOK

Within each topic is a brief textual description of the feature and possibly a Quick Tips section that provides a listing of associated features, buttons, and any keyboard shortcuts.

The secondary headers are the most common tasks associated with the topic, containing step-by-step instructions to complete the task.

Tips will be provided as necessary for each topic, but kept at a minimum. This is because the entire book is primarily a tip.

The final header in a topic tells you where to go for related information (**Tables**, for example, might refer you to **Columns** and/or **Borders**).

HOW TO USE THIS BOOK

Because this is an alphabetical listing, additional headers may be added for commonly looked up topics that fall under different topic titles. For example, it would be *common sense* to look up **Clipboard** for the new Excel 2000 Clipboard toolbar, but the *logical* place to cover the clipboard is when you are performing a **Copy and Cut** or **Paste**.

In addition, dialog box options and menu commands are in **bold type**. This is to show you that what you see in the book, you should see onscreen as well. Buttons that you need to click are displayed inline with regular text, to help you know exactly what to click on. Menu commands are listed as follows:

Choose **File**, **Print**.

This means that you click the word **File** on the menu bar and then click the **Print** command on the File menu.

ACCEPT OR REJECT CHANGES

When you are ready to finalize any tracked changes that have been made to a worksheet, you need to determine which changes you want to accept or reject. If you accept a change, Excel keeps it. If you reject a change, Excel restores the previous value and deletes the tracked change.

Quick Tip		
Feature	Button	Keyboard Shortcut
Revision Marks Toggle	TRK	Ctrl+⬆Shift+E

Review Tracked Changes

1. Choose **Tools, Track Changes, Accept or Reject Changes**.

2. Click [OK] in the message box that tells you this action saves the workbook, if the workbook has not been changed since the last save.

3. Select the options in the list boxes for **Which changes**:

   - **When:** Review changes made during the amount of time you select.

   - **Who:** Review changes made by the person's name you select.

   - **Where:** Review changes made to a specific range of cells you select.

4. Click [OK] to accept the changes.

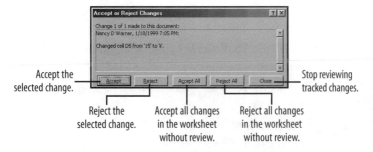

Accept the selected change.

Stop reviewing tracked changes.

Reject the selected change.

Accept all changes in the worksheet without review.

Reject all changes in the worksheet without review.

5. Click the appropriate button, as needed.

TIP

Move the mouse pointer over the cell with a comment marker to see a ScreenTip of the changes made, with information on who made the change and what the cell originally contained. Notice that the comment marker indicating a change made to a cell remains in the cell for your reference after you accept the change, but not if you reject the change.

Hide Changes Onscreen

1. Choose **Tools, Track Changes, Highlight Changes** to open the Highlight Changes dialog box.

2. Click to deselect the **Highlight changes on screen** option.

3. Click [OK] to accept the changes.

See Also Track Changes

ADD-INS

An add-in is a file that is loaded into Excel that provides additional macros, commands, or worksheet functionality. Some examples include different wizards that Excel provides you to load and use.

Load an Add-In

1. Choose **Tools, Add-Ins** to open the Add-Ins dialog box.

2. Click to select the **Add-Ins available** from the options Excel provides:

   - **Access Links:** Allows you to use Access forms and reports in Excel data tables.

   - **Analysis ToolPak:** Provides functions and interfaces for financial and scientific data analysis.

   - **Analysis ToolPak - VBA:** Provides VBA functions for financial and scientific data analysis.

   - **AutoSave Add-In:** Allows you to set a particular time interval for saving your workbooks.

- **Conditional Sum Wizard:** Walks you through summing data in lists.

- **Euro Currency Tools:** Converts and formats data for the Euro currency. This will actually add a **Euro** button on your Formatting toolbar.

- **Internet Assistant VBA:** Provides a VBA assistant for the Internet.

- **Lookup Wizard:** Walks you through creating formulas to find data in lists.

- **MS Query Add-In:** Allows MS Query macros the use of MS Query 1.0/2.0.

- **ODBC Add-In:** Provides functions for accessing SQL-based data sources with ODBC.

- **Report Manager:** Helps create reports by combining spreadsheet views with data scenarios.

- **Solver Add-In:** Provides tools for optimization and equation solving.

- **Template Utilities:** Provides supporting functions for Spreadsheet Solutions templates.

- **Template Wizard with Data Tracking:** Walks you through creating form templates with data tracking.

- **Update Add-In Links:** Updates links to Excel 4.0 add-in functions integrated in Excel.

3. Click [OK] to load the add-in. You can access the add-ins through the menu commands in Excel. The following list shows you which add-ins are found under each menu:

- View menu—Report Manager

- Tools menu—AutoSave, Solver, Data Analysis (Analysis ToolPack and Analysis ToolPack - VBA), Wizard (Conditional Sum and Lookup), and Update Add-In Links

- Data menu—Template Wizard, MS Access Form, MS Access Report, and Convert to MS Access

> **TIP**
>
> If you need to free up memory, you can unload the add-in, though it isn't removed from your computer or deleted, it can be added in again later.

Unload an Add-In

1. Choose **Tools, Add-Ins** to open the Add-Ins dialog box.
2. Click to deselect the **Add-Ins available** for the option(s) you want to remove.
3. Click [OK] to accept the changes and return to the worksheet.

See Also Analysis ToolPack, Templates

ALIGNMENT

When you enter data into a worksheet, numbers align to the left and text aligns to the right. However, you can change the alignment of data at any time, before or after you have entered the data.

Quick Tip

Feature	Button	Keyboard Shortcut
Merge & Center	⊞	
Align Left	▤	Ctrl+L
Align Right	▤	Ctrl+R
Center	▤	Ctrl+E
Increase Indent	▣	
Decrease Indent	▣	

Apply Text Alignment Control

1. Select the cell(s) that you want to format.

2. Choose **Format, Cells, Alignment** tab and select the options from the Format Cells dialog box.

Change the horizontal alignment between left, center, right, and justify.

Indent cell contents the number of characters to the right.

Change the vertical alignment between top, center, bottom, and justify.

Rotate text the selected degree.

Reduce the data's font to fit the column width.

Wrap text within the column width to see multiple lines.

Combine multiple selected cells into one cell.

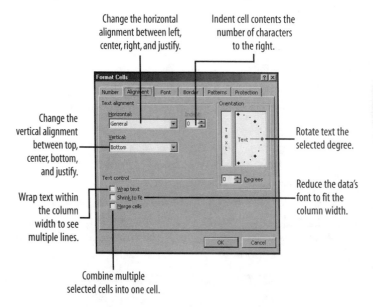

3. Click [OK] to accept changes and return to the worksheet.

TIP

You undo a set of merged and centered cells by first selecting the set of cells that are merged. Choose **Format, Cells**. Then click the **Alignment** tab and click the **Merge Cells** check box to deselect this option.

TIP

You can alter the alignment of text and data that has been wrapped within a cell. Sometimes this gives a cleaner look to your information.

See Also Fonts, Format, Text

ANALYSIS TOOLPACK

This add-in provides Excel with specialized analytical tools and worksheet functions for complex statistical and engineering analysis.

Use the Analysis ToolPack

1. Make sure that the Analysis ToolPack add-in is loaded in Excel (refer to the section "Add-Ins" for more information).

2. Choose **Tools, Data Analysis** to open the Data Analysis dialog box and choose from the various analysis tools.

3. Click an option from the **Analysis Tools** list and click ⬛ OK ⬛. The dialog box that corresponds with the analysis tool opens in which you can specify **Input** and **Output options**.

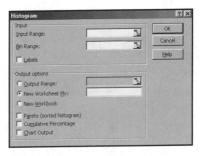

4. Type the **Input Range** and **Output Range** for the data analysis and click ⬛ OK ⬛. This is an example of the **Histogram** analysis tool. The analysis proceeds and the result appears in the designated output area.

See Also Add-Ins

AUDITING

Excel provides you with auditing tools to help you find and correct errors in your workbooks. This can be convenient when working with large worksheets where it is difficult to trace calculation precedents (locate cells used in the cell's calculation) and dependents (cell location of the calculation the current cell is used in).

Quick Tip	
Feature	*Keyboard Shortcut*
Direct Precedents	Ctrl + [
All Precedents	Ctrl + Shift + [
Direct Dependents	Ctrl +]
All Dependents	Ctrl + Shift +]

Trace Precedents

1. Click in the cell where there is a calculation error, or possibly just a calculation you want to review (data that precedes the calculation).

2. Choose **Tools, Auditing, Trace Precedents** to display arrows showing the cells that contain the data in the calculation.

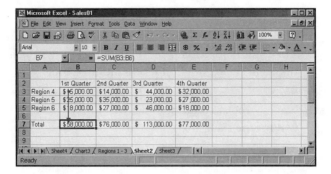

3. Choose **Tools, Auditing, Remove All Arrows** to remove the trace arrows.

TIP

Double-click the arrows to move from one reference to another.

Trace Dependents

1. Click in a cell where you want to see how the data is used in a calculation (data that is a dependent in a calculation).

2. Choose **Tools, Auditing, Trace Dependents** to display arrows showing where the cell data is used in a calculation.

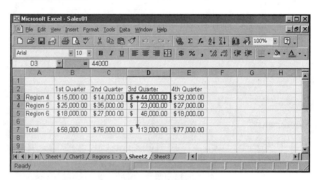

3. Choose **Tools, Auditing, Remove All Arrows** to remove the trace arrows.

Fix Errors

1. Click in a cell where there is a calculation error.

2. Choose **Tools, Auditing, Trace Error** to display arrows showing where the cell data comes from in the calculation. This helps you find where the error could be located.

3. Choose **Tools, Auditing, Remove All Arrows** to remove the trace arrows.

TIP

Instead of using the **Tools, Auditing** submenu each time you want to trace a precedent or dependent, you can choose **Tools, Auditing, Show Auditing Toolbar** and access the commands from the toolbar.

See Also Data Lists, Error Messages

AUTOCALCULATE

Use AutoCalculate to perform a calculation on data
without adding the function directly into the worksheet.

Use AutoCalculate

1. Select the cells you want to AutoCalculate.

2. Right-click the AutoCalculate section of the status
   bar (the default is the SUM function) and choose a
   type of calculation from the shortcut menu. Excel
   automatically calculates the cells and displays the
   answer in the status bar.

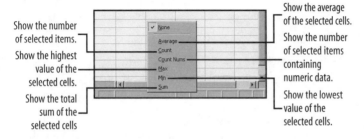

Show the number
of selected items.

Show the highest
value of the
selected cells.

Show the total
sum of the
selected cells

Show the average
of the selected cells.

Show the number
of selected items
containing
numeric data.

Show the lowest
value of the
selected cells.

See Also AutoSum, Formulas, Functions

AUTOCOMPLETE

Excel tries to automatically complete the entries you make
into a cell based on entries that have already been made in
a column or row.

Use AutoComplete

1. Type some text or values into a number of cells in a
   column.

2. Type text or a value into the cell below these entries;
   Excel tries to recognize the entry and list the text or
   value that would complete the entry according to the
   entries already listed in that column.

3. Press ⏎Enter if the value is correct, or continue typing
   the entry if it isn't correct.

Turn AutoComplete Off and On

1. Choose **Tools, Options; Edit** tab.
2. Click to deselect the **Enable AutoComplete for cell values** check box if you want to disable this feature; select the check box to enable this feature.

See Also AutoFill

AUTOCORRECT

Excel 2000 enables you to automatically correct yourself if you find you continue to make the same typing errors in your worksheets. The most common errors to automatically correct are capitalization options, spelling checker corrections, and AutoCorrect entries.

Replace Text As You Type

1. Choose **Tools, AutoCorrect** and click the **Replace text as you type** check box (if not already selected by default).
2. Type the text you commonly spell incorrectly in the **Replace** text box. Type the correct text in the **With** text box.

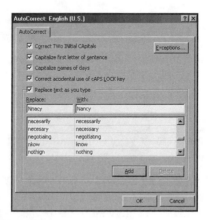

3. Click [Add] to add an automatic correction.
4. Click [OK] to accept your changes.

Delete a Replace Text As You Type Option

1. Choose **Tools, AutoCorrect**; scroll through and click the **Replace text as you type** option you want to delete.

2. Click ⬚ Delete ⬚ and then click ⬚ OK ⬚ to accept your changes.

AutoCorrect Exceptions

1. Choose **Tools, AutoCorrect** and then click ⬚Exceptions...⬚; **First Letter** tab.

2. Type the text you commonly type in the **Don't capitalize after** text box and click ⬚ Add ⬚. You can also select an option in the list box and click ⬚ Delete ⬚ to remove it.

3. Click the text you commonly type in the **Don't correct** text box of the **INitial CAps** tab and click ⬚ Add ⬚. You can also select an option in the list box and click ⬚ Delete ⬚ to remove it.

4. Click the ⬚ OK ⬚ button in both dialog boxes to accept your changes and return to the workbook.

Deselect AutoCorrect Options

1. Choose **Tools, AutoCorrect**; **AutoCorrect** tab.

2. Click to deselect each AutoCorrect option you don't want to use:

   - Correct TWo INitial CApitals
   - Capitalize first letter of sentences
   - Capitalize names of days
   - Correct accidental usage of cAPS LOCK key
   - Replace text as you type

3. Click ⬚ OK ⬚ to accept your changes.

See Also AutoComplete, AutoFormat, Spelling

AUTOFILL

AutoFill can automatically extend series types like dates, quarters, periods, and even number trends. For example, instead of typing all the months in a different cell in a column, type in the first two months and have Excel complete the rest of the cells.

Use AutoFill

1. Type the first two cell entries for a series of data (or enough cells to start a text or number trend).
2. Click the pointer on the bottom-right cell corner when it becomes a plus sign.
3. Drag the pointer to the number of cells in the series.

See Also Move Data, Copy and Cut, Paste

AUTOFORMAT

Excel helps you format your data and worksheets quickly with an AutoFormat feature. With AutoFormat, you save valuable time by having Excel apply preset colors and fonts and predefined formats to your worksheets to give them a professional look in a fraction of the time.

AutoFormat

1. Select the cells you want to AutoFormat.
2. Choose **Format, AutoFormat** to open the AutoFormat dialog box.
3. Scroll through the Table format list box and view previews of the formats in the sample preview area.
4. Click the format you prefer and then click ▭ OK ▭ to apply the AutoFormat to your data.

TIP

Even after you have selected a table AutoFormat, you can determine different formats to apply to the selected table. Click [Options...] to select and deselect the **Formats to apply** and **Apply special formats to** options.

See Also Conditional Formatting, Fonts, Text

AUTOSHAPES

Excel provides shapes that can be automatically inserted into worksheets, so that you don't have to create them from scratch. This is convenient when you want to use a graphic to draw attention to something on a report.

Insert AutoShapes

1. Click the ⬛ button on the Formatting toolbar to open the Drawing toolbar at the bottom of the worksheet.

2. Click [AutoShapes ▾] and select the particular shape you want to add to your worksheet from the submenu.

3. Click in the worksheet and drag the crosshatch pointer to the desired shape size.

Change AutoShapes

1. Click the ⬛ button on the Formatting toolbar to open the Drawing toolbar at the bottom of the worksheet.

2. Click directly on the AutoShape you entered in your worksheet.

3. Click **Draw, Change AutoShape** on the Drawing toolbar and select a different shape.

Format AutoShapes

1. Right-click the AutoShape you entered in your worksheet and choose **Format AutoShape** from the shortcut menu.

2. Select the following tabs to choose options for formatting your AutoShape:

   - **Colors and Lines**—You can change the color that fills in the AutoShape and display particular types of lines around the AutoShape.

   - **Size**—You can size and rotate the AutoShape as well as alter the scale.

   - **Layout**—You can alter the wrapping style of the AutoShape (how text is flowed around or over the object) and the alignment of the AutoShape in the document.

   - **Web**—You can type the text you want to display while a Web browser is loading the AutoShape.

3. Click [OK] on any of the tabs to accept changes and return to the document.

TIP

Click the 🖉 button on the Standard toolbar to toggle between displaying and hiding the Drawing toolbar.

See Also Clip Art, Drawing Tools, WordArt

AUTOSUM

Excel can use formulas to perform calculations for you. Because a formula refers to the cells rather than to the values, Excel updates the sum whenever you change the values in the cells.

Use AutoSum

1. Click in the cell where you want the total of a range of cells to be added.

2. Click the ⟨Σ⟩ button on the Standard toolbar. Excel automatically selects the most obvious range of numbers to calculate. You can also select the range of cells in advance and the calculation will be placed the next cell over or below the selection. If that cell isn't available, it will place the calculation at the closest end of the selected row or column of cells.

3. Press ⟨↵Enter⟩ to accept the range. The formula for the calculated cells is displayed in the Formula bar.

See Also AutoCalculate, Formulas, Functions

AVERAGE

The average function is one of Excel's many built-in formulas for performing a specialized calculation on the data in your worksheet. It will find the average number of a range of cells.

Enter an Average Function

1. Click the cell where you want the result of the function to appear.

2. Click the ⟨ƒ⟩ button on the Standard toolbar to open the Paste Function dialog box.

3. Double-click the **AVERAGE** option in the **Most Recently Used Function Category, Function Name** list box. Excel selects a range of cells it determines you want to average and places it in the Average Function box.

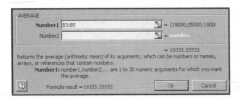

4. Accept the range or type the cell range or range name you want and click ⟨ OK ⟩ . The result appears in the active cell and the function is displayed in the Formula bar.

> **TIP**
>
> If Excel doesn't automatically select the cells you want, you can select them yourself by clicking in the first cell, holding down (⬆Shift), and clicking in the last cell.

See Also COUNTIF, MAX, MIN, SUMIF

AXIS
see Charts   pg 19

BACKGROUNDS

You can apply a background file to your worksheet to add visual interest.

Apply a Worksheet Background

1. Choose **Format**, **Sheet**, **Background** to open the Format Sheet Background dialog box.

2. Click the **Places bar** option (History, My Documents, Desktop, Favorites, or Web Folders) for the location of the background file you want to open.

3. Click the **Look in** drop-down list box to help locate the correct file or drive. You can also click the 🖻 button to move through folders.

4. Double-click the file you want to open and Excel opens the workbook.

Delete a Background

Choose **Format**, **Sheet**, **Delete Background** to remove the background applied to a worksheet.

> **TIP**
>
> Office clip art, Windows wallpaper, and even graphics that you have created can serve as backgrounds.

See Also Clip Art, Patterns, Watermarks, WordArt

BOLD

see Format   pg 61; Fonts   pg 59

BORDERS

You can add a border to any or all sides of a cell, selected
cells, or objects. In addition, you can format the types and
styles of borders for your data.

A
B
C

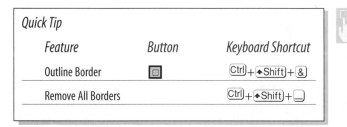

Quick Tip

Feature	Button	Keyboard Shortcut
Outline Border	▣	Ctrl + ◆Shift + &
Remove All Borders		Ctrl + ◆Shift + ▭

Add Text Borders

1. Select the cell or cells to which you want to add a border.

2. Click ▣ on the Formatting toolbar and select how you
   want the border applied from the drop-down list.

Format Borders

1. Select the cells that have a border you want to format.

2. Choose **Format, Cells; Border** tab.

3. Select the optional **Presets, Line Style** and **Color**, and
   Border settings in the preview diagram.

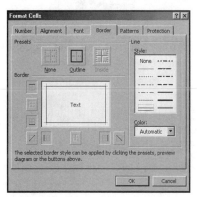

4. Click [ok] to accept changes and return to the worksheet.

See Also Cells, Format, Graphics, Print, Shading

CELLS

A worksheet is a grid of columns and rows. The intersection of a column and a row is called a cell. Each cell in a worksheet has a unique cell reference, the designation formed by combining the row and column headings.

Quick Tip	
Feature	*Keyboard Shortcut*
Insert Blank Cells	Ctrl + ↑Shift + +
Delete Selection	Ctrl + -

Insert Cells

1. Select the cell(s) where you want to insert new cell(s) above or to the left of your existing data.

2. Choose **Insert, Cells** to open the Insert dialog box.

3. Select an **Insert** option and click [ok] to accept changes and return to the worksheet.

Delete Cells and Cell Content

1. Select the cell(s) you want to delete; meaning that you want to remove the cell(s) and shift the cells around it in addition to the contents of the cells.

2. Choose **Edit, Delete** to open the Delete dialog box.

3. Select a **Delete** option and click [___ OK ___] to accept changes and return to the worksheet.

Delete Cell Content Only

1. Select the cell(s) you want to clear; meaning that you want to remove the contents of the cell(s) and not shift the cells around it.

2. Choose **Edit**, **Clear**, and choose whether you want to clear the cell **Comments**, **Contents**, **Formats**, or **All** from the submenu.

TIP

When you delete the contents of a cell, Excel automatically updates any formulas affected by the insertion. This might cause calculation errors, see the section on "Auditing" for more information.

Replace Cell Data

1. Select the cell that contains the data you want to replace.

2. Type the new cell data and press [←Enter]. The formatting already assigned to the cell remains, but the data is replaced.

See Also Alignment, Columns, Fonts, Numbers, Rows

CHARTS

Numeric data can sometimes be difficult to interpret. Using that data to create charts helps the reader visualize the data's significance. Excel provides you with a Chart Wizard to interpret your data and assist you in creating charts. You can quickly change the appearance of charts in Excel by clicking directly on the chart. You can change titles, legend information, axis points, category names, and more.

Quick Tip		
Feature	*Button*	*Keyboard Shortcut*
Chart Wizard	🔳	
Create Chart		F11
Insert Chart Sheet		Alt + F1

Create a Chart

1. Select the cells you want to include in the chart.

2. Click the 🔳 button on the Standard toolbar.

3. Click the **Chart type** and **Chart sub-type** in the Chart Wizard dialog box, then choose Next >.

4. Click **Rows** (or **Columns**) to choose on which data the chart will be based, then choose Next >. You can also change the data range in, if you selected too many, not enough, or the wrong cells.

5. Type the various **Titles** for the chart, then choose Next >.

6. Click the option for where you want to place the chart, then choose Finish.

Plot Area   Chart Area

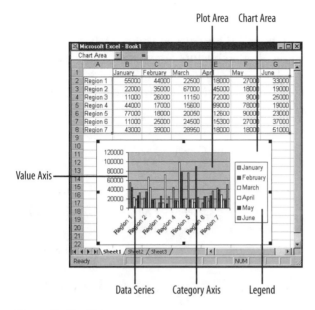

Value Axis

Data Series   Category Axis   Legend

Change the Chart Type

1. Right-click the Plot Area and choose **Chart Type** from the shortcut menu.

2. Select the alternate **Chart type** and **Chart sub-type** you want in the Chart Type dialog box.

3. Click [OK]. The updated chart type appears in the chart.

Alter Source Data Range

1. Right-click the Plot Area and choose **Source Data** from the shortcut menu.

2. Click directly in your worksheet and select the data range you want. The **Data range** area is automatically updated with the cells you selected.

3. Click [OK]. The updated data range appears in your chart.

Alter Chart Options

1. Right-click the Plot Area and choose **Chart Options** from the shortcut menu to open the Chart Options dialog box. Any changes you make to this dialog box automatically appear in the chart preview window in the dialog box.

2. Click the following tabs to alter options on your chart:

   - **Titles:** Alter the **Chart title** and different axis options.

   - **Axes:** Alter the **Primary Axis** on your chart.

   - **Gridlines:** Add **Category (X) axis** and **Value (Y) axis Major** and **Minor gridlines** to your chart.

   - **Legend:** Alter the **Placement** of the legend in your chart.

   - **Data Labels:** Alter the **Data Labels** to be more or less descriptive.

   - **Data Table:** Select to **Show Data Table** with your chart.

3. Click [OK] to accept all your chart options. This takes you back to your main worksheet where you can see how your chart has changed.

TIP

To change the pattern and scale of the gridlines, double-click on a gridline itself. Then use the Format Gridlines dialog box to make your selections and click [OK].

Format the Plot Area

1. Right-click the Plot Area and choose **Format Plot Area** from the shortcut menu.

2. Select the **Area color, Fill Effects,** and **Border** on the **Patterns** tab of the Format Plot Area dialog box.

3. Click [OK] to accept your changes and return to the chart.

> **TIP**
>
> If you are unsure whether you are in the Chart Area or the Plot Area, move the mouse pointer directly over that particular area of the chart. A ScreenTip appears, telling you in which area you are. Or, you can click directly on the chart and refer to the Name Box below the Font drop-down list box.

Format the Chart Area

1. Right-click the **Chart Area** and choose **Format Chart Area** from the shortcut menu.

2. Click the **Font** tab of the Format Plot Area dialog box.

3. Select the **Font** options you would prefer.

4. Click the **Patterns** tab and select a type of **Border** around the chart and any color or **Fill Effects** you want for the chart **Area** itself.

5. Click [OK] to accept your changes and return to the chart.

Format the Value Axis Scale

1. Right-click the **Value Axis** and choose **Format Axis** from the shortcut menu.

2. Click the **Scale** tab of the Format Axis dialog box.

3. Type different units for the following values (the Auto values are determined by Microsoft Graph):

   - **Minimum:** Displays the lowest value from all data series.

   - **Maximum:** Displays the highest value from all data series.

   - **Major Unit:** Choose the major tick mark and gridline intervals.

   - **Minor Unit:** Choose the minor tick mark and gridline intervals.

   - **Category (X) axis crosses at:** Select where to cross the value and category axis.

4. Click [OK] to accept your changes and return to the chart.

TIP

If you notice that one of the data points in your chart is way off scale, this is a good sign that you might have entered data into your worksheet incorrectly. If this is the case, simply edit the worksheet data; the chart updates automatically. Also refer to the task on altering the original data.

Format the Category Axis Scale

1. Right-click the **Category Axis** and choose **Format Axis** from the shortcut menu.

2. Click the **Scale** tab of the Format Axis dialog box.

3. Type a number in the **Value (Y) axis crosses at category number** to specify the category number where you want the value (y) axis to cross the category (x) axis.

4. Type a number in the **Number of categories between tick marks labels** to specify the frequency at which you want categories on the category (x) axis to be labeled.

5. Type a number in the **Number of categories between tick marks** to specify the frequency at which you want categories on the category (x) axis.

6. Select from the following options:

   - **Value (Y) axis crosses between categories:** Plots data points between tick marks, otherwise plotted at the tick marks.

   - **Categories in reverse order:** Reverses the order that the categories on the (x) axis are displayed.

   - **Value (Y) axis crosses at maximum category:** Crosses the (y) axis after the last category on the (x) axis.

7. Click [OK] to accept your changes and return to the chart.

Alter the Original Data

1. Select the worksheet or range that contains the charted data.

2. Click a cell that you want to alter or need to update.

3. Type in the new data and press (↵Enter).

4. Click back to the chart to accept your changes and return to the chart.

See Also Cells, Format, Numbers, Workspace

CLIP ART

Clip art adds visual interest to your Excel worksheets. You can choose from numerous types of prepared images.

Insert Clip Art

1. Choose **Insert, Picture, Clip Art** to open the Insert Clip Art dialog box.

2. Click on the **Categories** of clip art in the Pictures tab and scroll through the options. At the bottom of the list of clip art is a **Keep Looking** link that enables you to view more clips.

3. Click on the piece of clip art and choose [🖼] from the pop-up menu. This inserts the clip art into your worksheet.

4. Click the [✕] button to close the Insert Clip Art dialog box.

Forward to
viewed clips.

View all clip
categories.

Back to
previous
clips.

Change to
small window.

Paste clip in
location.

Insert clip.
Preview clip.
Add clip
to another
category.

Copy clip to
clipboard.
Find similar
clips.
View more clips
in a category.

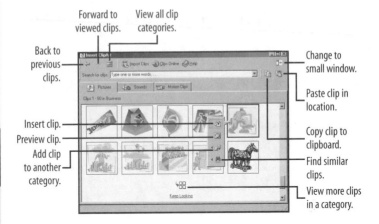

Format Clip Art

1. Right-click the clip art you entered in your document and choose **Format Picture** from the shortcut menu.

2. Select the following tabs to choose options for formatting your clip art:

   - **Colors and Lines:** Change the color that fills in the clip art.

   - **Size:** Size and rotate the clip art as well as alter the scale.

   - **Layout:** Alter the wrapping style of the clip art (how text is flowed around or over the object) and the alignment of the clip art in the document.

   - **Picture:** Set the crop size of the object and control the color, brightness, and object contrast.

   - **Web:** Alter the text displayed when this graphic is loading on a Web page.

3. Click [OK] to accept changes and return to the document.

See Also Borders, Drawing Tools

CLIPBOARD
see Copy and Cut   pg 33; Paste   pg 101

CLOSE

When you finish working in a workbook, you can close it and continue to work on other workbooks. You can close a file with or without saving changes. Note that this is different than exiting the application.

Quick Tip		
Feature	*Button*	*Keyboard Shortcut*
Close Worksheet	⊠	Ctrl+F4 or Ctrl+W

Close a Workbook

1. Click the ⊠ button. If you have changed the workbook, Excel asks you whether you want to save it.

2. Click `Yes` to save changes and close the worksheet. Click `No` to close the worksheet without saving changes. Click `Cancel` to return to working in your worksheet without closing it.

See Also Exit, Save Worksheets

COLOR
see Patterns   pg 103

COLUMNS

Columns are a vertical set of cells in a worksheet labeled with letters.

Quick Tip	
Feature	*Keyboard Shortcut*
Hide Columns	Ctrl+0
Unhide Columns	Ctrl+⬆Shift+)

A
B
C

Insert Columns

1. Select a cell near the place you want to add a new column. The inserted column is placed to the left of the selected cell.

2. Choose **Insert, Columns** to insert the column.

Delete Columns

1. Click the column heading of the column you want to delete.

2. Right-click and choose **Delete** from the shortcut menu.

Hide Columns

1. Click to select the column you want to hide.

2. Choose **Format, Column, Hide** to hide the column. Or, you can simply click and drag the right border of a column past the left border of the column.

TIP

Hidden elements don't print when you print the worksheet.

Unhide Columns

1. Select the columns on both sides of the column you want to unhide.

2. Choose **Format, Column, Unhide** to display the hidden column.

Format Columns

1. Select a cell in the column you want to format.

2. Choose **Format, Column,** and select the appropriate option from the submenu.

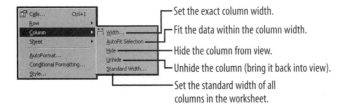

Set the exact column width.

Fit the data within the column width.

Hide the column from view.

Unhide the column (bring it back into view).

Set the standard width of all columns in the worksheet.

TIP

To make multiple columns the same width, click the mouse and drag over all the column headers you want resized. Then resize one of the columns. Each highlighted column becomes that size.

TIP

To automatically make a column fit the width of the widest cell, choose **Format, Column, AutoFit**.

See Also Cells, Freezing Panes, Rows, Workspace

COMMENTS

When working in a workbook, you might find that you need to add a note reminding yourself to verify information when you work on the workbook later. Or, perhaps you are sharing workbooks with other users and want to keep track of the comments that each user makes.

Insert Comments

1. Select the cell where you want to place a comment, or place the cursor at the location where you want to insert a comment.

2. Choose **Insert, Comment** to open the comment text box.

3. Type the comment and click in the worksheet when you're finished. Notice that the cell's upper-right corner is now colored to indicate the comment.

> **TIP**
>
> Move the mouse pointer over the highlighted comment indicator and the comment appears in a ScreenTip.

View All Comments

1. Choose **View, Comments** to toggle between viewing all the worksheet comment text boxes. Notice that the Reviewing toolbar appears.

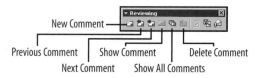

2. Click the **Close** ⊠ button to close the Reviewing toolbar.

Edit Comments

1. Right-click the commented cell and choose **Edit Comment** from the shortcut menu.
2. Type the changes into the comment text box and click in the worksheet when finished.

> **TIP**
>
> You can quickly add, edit, or delete a comment by right-clicking the mouse on the cell that contains the comment marker and selecting the correct command from the shortcut menu.

See Also Track Changes, Share and Protect Worksheets

CONDITIONAL FORMAT

At times, you might want the formatting of a cell to depend on the value it contains. The Conditional Formatting feature enables you to specify up to three conditions that, when met, cause the cell to be formatted in the manner defined for that condition. If none of the conditions is met, the cell keeps its original formatting.

Apply Conditional Formatting

1. Select the cells you want to format conditionally.

2. Choose **Format, Conditional Formatting** to open the Conditional Formatting dialog box.

3. Click the **Condition** 1 drop-down list to select whether the condition is for a cell value or a formula.

Indicate the type of operator.   Condition(s) to be met.

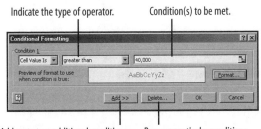

Add up to two additional conditions.   Remove particular conditions.

4. Click the operator drop-down list box to the right of **Condition** 1, which you can use to set the condition of the format values.

5. Type the value of the condition(s) to be met.

6. Click [Format...] to set the format to use when the condition is met.

7. Click the options you want to set in the Format Cells dialog box.

8. Click [OK] to accept your formatting conditions.

9. Click the [OK] button in the Conditional Formatting dialog box. Excel applies your formatting to any cells that meet the condition you specified.

TIP

You can copy the conditional formatting from one cell to another by using the 🖅 button. Click the cell whose formatting you want to duplicate. Then click the 🖅 button. Finally, drag over the cells to which you want to apply the formatting.

See Also AutoFormat

CONSOLIDATE

Consolidating summarizes the data from one or more source areas and displays it in a table or cell. For example, you can consolidate the data from two columns into on different column, perhaps if you wanted to sum the cells but not make the destination cells a calculation formula.

Consolidate Data

1. Click in the cells, or in one cell if you like, where you want your data to be consolidated.

2. Choose **Data, Consolidate** to open the Consolidate dialog box.

3. Click the **Function** drop-down list to select how you want the consolidated data to be calculated.

4. Click the **Reference Collapse** dialog box button and select the range of the first set of data you want to consolidate.

5. Click the **Reference Expand** dialog box button and click [Add] to add the data range to the **All references** list box.

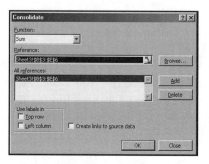

6. Repeat steps 4 and 5 for each set of data you want to consolidate.

7. Click [OK] to consolidate the data and review the results in the worksheet.

See Also Merge Workbooks

COPY AND CUT

You can share information within and between workbooks in Excel (and other Office applications) by copying and cutting cells and objects. You can now copy and cut up to 12 different items onto the Clipboard at a time. The Clipboard is where items are stored before you paste them.

Quick Tip		
Feature	*Button*	*Keyboard Shortcut*
Copy	📋	Ctrl+C or Ctrl+Insert
Copy Format	🖌	Ctrl+⬆Shift+C
Copy Text Only		⬆Shift+F2
Cut	✂	Ctrl+X or ⬆Shift+Del

Copy

1. Select the cells or object you want to copy.
2. Click the 📋 button on the Standard toolbar. The original text remains in this location and a copy is placed on the Clipboard, ready to be pasted.

Cut

1. Select the text or object you want to cut.
2. Click the ✂ button on the Standard toolbar. This removes the text from its original location and places it on the clipboard, ready to be pasted.

Copy Multiple Items

1. Choose **View, Toolbars, Clipboard** to open the new Clipboard toolbar.
2. Select an item you want to copy and then click the 📋 button on the Clipboard toolbar. Repeat this process each time you select an item (up to 12 items). You can also use the original 📋 and ✂ buttons on the Standard toolbar to place items on the Clipboard toolbar.

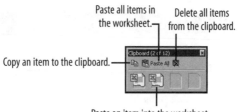

Paste all items in the worksheet. / Delete all items from the clipboard.

Copy an item to the clipboard.

Paste an item into the worksheet.

3. Move the mouse pointer over the items on the Clipboard toolbar and a ScreenTip displays what is contained in each copied clip (unless the clip is extensive, in which case only part of it will display).

4. Move the mouse pointer to where you want to insert the text or object. Click the clip to paste the item in the worksheet.

TIP

The Clipboard toolbar automatically appears after you click the 🗷 or 🗷 button multiple times. Click the 🗷 button to close the Clipboard toolbar, or choose **View, Toolbars, Clipboard** to toggle the toolbar closed.

Copy Formulas

1. Select the cell(s) with the formula that you want to copy.

2. Click the 🗷 button on the Standard toolbar. The original text remains in this location and a copy is placed on the Clipboard ready to be pasted.

3. Click in the cell(s) where you want the formula to be copied.

4. Choose **Edit, Paste Special** to open the Paste Special dialog box.

5. Click the **Formulas** option in the **Paste** area and click ⬚ OK ⬚ to return to the worksheet. The formula appears in the cell(s).

See Also Error Messages, Format Painter, Move Data, Objects, Paste

COUNT

The count function is one of Excel's many built-in formulas for performing a specialized calculation on the data in your worksheet. It finds the total number of cells in a range of data.

Count Cells

1. Click the cell where you want the result of the function to appear.

2. Click the 🔳 button on the Standard toolbar to open the Paste Function dialog box.

3. Double-click the **COUNT** option in the **Most Recently Used Function Category**, **Function Name** list box. Excel opens the Count function box and automatically inserts what it considers the most likely Value1 argument to be counted based on the cell that you have chosen for your results.

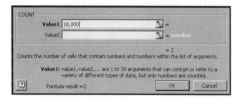

4. Accept this argument or type the Value1 argument you want, press (Tab↹), and type any other Value arguments (up to 30), and then click ⬚ᴼᴷ⬚. The result appears in the active cell and the function is displayed in the Formula bar.

TIP

If Excel doesn't automatically select the cells you want, you can select them yourself by clicking in the first cell, holding down (◆Shift), and clicking in the last cell.

See Also AutoCalculate, COUNTIF, Functions

COUNTIF

The countif function is one of Excel's many built-in formulas for performing a specialized calculation on the data in your worksheet. It finds the total number of cells that meet a set of requirements in a range of data.

Count Cells If They Meet Criteria

1. Click the cell where you want the result of the function to appear.

2. Click the ☒ button on the Standard toolbar to open the Paste Function dialog box.

3. Double-click the **COUNTIF** option in the **Most Recently Used Function Category**, **Function Name** list box. Excel automatically inserts what it considers the most likely range to be counted if they meet your criteria based on the cell that you have chosen for your results.

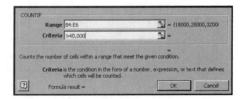

4. Accept this range or type in the **Range** you want, press [Tab⇆] and type the **Criteria**, and then click [OK]. The result appears in the active cell and the function is displayed in the Formula bar.

TIP

If Excel doesn't automatically select the cells you want, you can select them yourself by clicking in the first cell, holding down [◆Shift], and clicking in the last cell.

See Also AVERAGE, MAX, MIN, SUMIF

CURRENCY

see Numbers   pg 88

CUSTOM VIEWS

You can create custom views for your worksheet files to save different ways of displaying, printing, and viewing your worksheets without saving them as separate files.

Create and Use a Custom View

1. Choose **View, Custom Views** to open the Custom View dialog box.

2. Click [Add...] to add a new view.

3. Type a view **Name** and select whether you want to save the **Print settings** and/or **Hidden rows, columns and filter settings**.

4. Click [OK] to accept changes and return to the worksheet. Save your workbook and change the view of your current worksheet, for example, by altering the Zoom percentage. This will change your current view.

5. Choose **View, Custom Views** to open the Custom View dialog box.

6. Click the optional view from the **Views** list and click [Show]. The worksheet workspace automatically appears as you save the custom view.

See Also Workspace

DATA LISTS

Excel is for more than just totaling numbers. You can also use the program as a simple data management program. Or, you might use it to keep track of clients, products, orders, and expenses. You can set up a data list, enter data into a form, and use some of Excel's data list features, which include:

- **Data Validation:** Set up rules for the format and type of data that can be entered as a record into a data list form.
- **Find Records:** Locate records in a data list form.
- **Modify Records:** Alter records in data list form.
- **Delete Records:** Remove records in a data list form.
- **Sort Data List:** Organize all records in a data list in a specific order.
- **Filter Data List:** View only the records in a data list that meet specific criteria.
- **Subtotal Data List:**

Set Up a Data List Form

1. Type the heading names for each column of information. Select all the headers and format them. Format any other cells as necessary (refer to the "Format" section for additional information).

2. Select the cells in which you want to establish your data list.

3. Choose **Data, Form**. This tells Excel that you want the selected cells to be used as the data form labels. The form appears, ready for you to enter data.

TIP

Be sure to use unique names for each column. Excel becomes confused if you use the same name for more than one column.

Enter Data with a Form

1. Place your active cell within the data list and choose **Data, Form** to open the data form for the worksheet data list.

2. Type the data for the first record into the data form pressing (Tab⇆) between each field on the form.

3. Click [New] on the data list form. The data is automatically placed in your data list and the data form is ready for another entry.

4. Click [Close] on the form to return to working in your worksheet data list.

TIP

You can close the data list form by clicking [Close] on the form.

Apply Data Validation

1. Click a cell anywhere in the selected data list to which you want to apply data validation. The cells are now considered *fields* in the data list.

2. Choose **Data, Validation; Settings** tab to open the Data Validation dialog box.

3. Click a **Validation criteria** option from the **Allow** drop-down list box.

Specify a list of   Numbers or
valid entries.   fractions only   No restrictions   Integers only

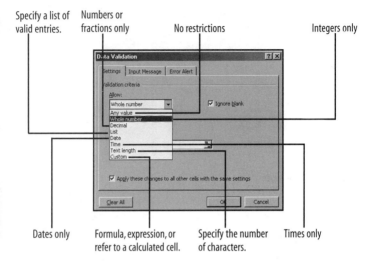

Dates only   Formula, expression, or   Specify the number   Times only
                refer to a calculated cell. of characters.

4. Click any necessary operators (i.e. between, equal to) from the **Data** drop-down list and type any restrictions (i.e. minimum, maximum) for the final validation criteria.

5. Click [OK] to accept your validation rules. This will utilize Excel's default validation error message when invalid data is entered. If you want to change the error message, see the tip at the end of this section.

TIP

You can alter the Excel default validation error message by choosing the **Error Alert** tab of the Data Validation dialog box. Here you can alter the error alert style, title, and error message. This is convenient when people who aren't familiar with your data list form enter incorrect data; you can tell them specifically what data they need to correct.

Test Data Validation

1. Type in a new data list record but add an incorrect entry in the validation field, then click [New]. Refer to the previous section "Enter Data with a Form," if you need help.

2. Click [Retry] on the error message to return to the invalid record entry.

3. Type a correct entry and click [New] again. The record is accepted.

TIP

In addition to validation rules and error messages, you can add input messages directly in your data list. This will look like a permanently viewable comment in your data list. Choose the **Input Message** tab of the Data Validation dialog box and type a **Title** and **Input Message** to show the user when a cell is selected that has data validation requirements applied to it.

Find a Record

1. Place your active cell within the data list and choose **Data, Form** to open the data form for the worksheet data list.

2. Click [Criteria]. The form becomes blank, awaiting your entry of the search criteria.

3. Type in the search criteria and click the [Find Next] button. Excel displays the first matching record. Continue clicking on [Find Next] until the record you want is displayed.

TIP

To open the data list form at any time, the active cell must be somewhere within the data list.

Modify a Record

1. Place your active cell within the data list and choose **Data, Form** to open the data form for the worksheet data list.

2. Find the record you want to modify using the Find a Record process explained in the preceding section.

3. Type the edits to the field and click [Close] to accept the change and return to the worksheet data list.

Delete Data Records

1. Place your active cell within the data list and choose **Data, Form** to open the data form for the worksheet data list.

2. Find the record you want to modify using the Find a Record process explained in the previous section.

3. Click [Delete] to permanently remove the record from the data list. Click [OK] in the message box if you want to permanently delete the record from the data list; click [Cancel] if you don't want to delete the record.

Sort a Data List

1. Place your active cell within the data list and choose **Data, Sort** to open the Sort dialog box.

2. Click the field name from the **Sort by** drop-down list and select **Ascending** or **Descending** order for the first sort criteria.

3. Click any other field names from either or both of the two **Then by** drop-down lists and select **Ascending** or **Descending** order for the sort criteria.

4. Click [OK] and Excel will sort the entire data list.

Filter a Data List

1. Place your active cell within the data list and choose **Data, Filter, AutoFilter** to add drop-down arrows to each field header.

2. Click the arrow next to the field you want to use for the filtering criteria.

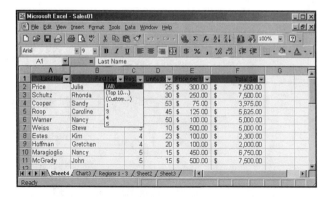

3. Select what filtering criteria you want to match. You can select a specific field in the record or a particular value:

- **All:** Display all the records in the data list.

- **Top 10:** Use the **Show** options in the Top 10 AutoFilter dialog box to display the **Top** or **Bottom** 1 through **500 Items**; or display the **Top** or **Bottom** **Percentage**.

- **Custom:** Use the **Show rows where** options in the Custom AutoFilter dialog box to display records that may meet a set of criteria.

Excel is already displaying only those records that meet the selected criteria. You can tell the database has been filtered because the filter arrow is a different color.

TIP

To remove an AutoFilter, choose **Data, Filter, AutoFilter**. The arrows disappear and the entire data list is again visible.

Add Record Subtotals

1. Sort the data on the records you want to subtotal or use the entire data list. Refer to the section "Sort a Data List," for help.

2. Choose **Data, Subtotals** to open the Subtotal dialog box.

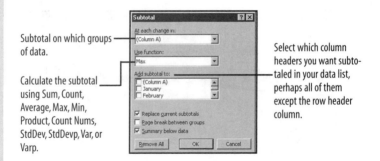

Subtotal on which groups of data.

Calculate the subtotal using Sum, Count, Average, Max, Min, Product, Count Nums, StdDev, StdDevp, Var, or Varp.

Select which column headers you want subtotaled in your data list, perhaps all of them except the row header column.

3. Click the **At each change in** drop-down list to select the specific column you want the subtotal grouped by.

4. Click the **Use function** drop-down list box to select how you want the subtotaled rows to be calculated.

5. Click each **Add subtotal to** option to indicate the column you want the subtotal calculated on.

6. Click ⬚⬚. Excel inserts a subtotal row for each time the selected field changes, performs the selected function on the column you asked to total, and adds a grand total at the end of the data list.

See Also Filter Data, Functions, Sort Data

DATA TABLE
see Tables   pg 131

DECIMALS

Excel lets you globally fix the number of decimal places when you enter a number into a cell. This way you don't have to press **increase decimal** each time you want to enter a decimal point.

Fix Decimal Places

1. Choose **Tools, Options; Edit** tab.

2. Click the **Fixed decimal** option and use the Places spin box to globally indicate the number of decimal places you want the cell to automatically insert.

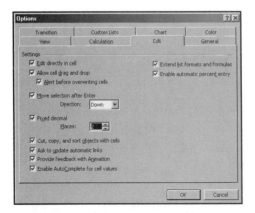

3. Click **OK** to accept changes and return to the worksheet.

4. Type a long number (**99999**) into a cell and press ⏎**Enter**; the number will automatically appear with the set number of decimal places (**999.99**).

TIP

You can change the decimal settings for individual cells or selected cells through either the toolbar or the formatting menu option. See the "Numbers" section for more information on increasing or decreasing decimal places.

See Also Numbers

DIV/0!
see Error Messages pg 50

DETECT AND REPAIR

Detect and repair automatically finds and fixes errors in your current session of Excel. When doing this, have your installation disks nearby and close any other applications you have open.

Run Detect and Repair

1. Choose **Help, Detect and Repair** in Excel.

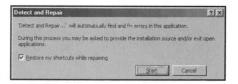

2. Click Start in the Detect and Repair dialog box. Note that the **Restore my shortcuts while repairing** check box adds the program shortcuts to the Windows Start menu, if selected.

3. Select the other application you are running and want to **Cancel**, **Retry**, or **Ignore**.

See Also Help, Office Assistant, Office on the Web

DIALOG BOXES

Windows uses dialog boxes to display information to and request input from the end user. The different ways you can provide input are through buttons, text boxes, option buttons (also known as radio buttons), check boxes, spin boxes, list boxes, and drop-down list boxes.

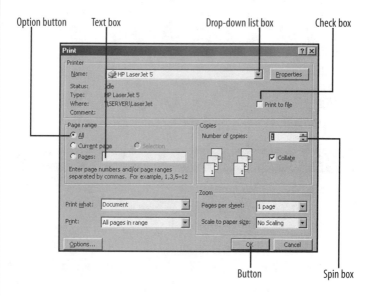

Get Help in a Dialog Box

1. Click the ☑ in the upper-right area of the dialog box title bar.

2. Click on the item you need help with and a ScreenTip appears with descriptive information.

3. Click anywhere on your desktop or press Esc to continue.

Close a Dialog Box with Changes

Click ⬚OK⬚ or press ↵Enter. Any changes made to the dialog box will be accepted and applied.

Close a Dialog Box Without Changes

Click ☒ in the upper-right corner on the dialog box title bar or press Esc. Any changes made to the dialog box will be lost unless you have already clicked ⬚Apply⬚.

TIP

If the dialog box has an ⬚Apply⬚ button to apply changes made in the dialog box, you still must exit the dialog box. To do so, you can also click ⬚Cancel⬚ or ⬚Close⬚.

See Also Menus, What's This?

DOCKED TOOLBAR
see Toolbars   pg 135

DRAG AND DROP
see Copy and Cut   pg 33

DRAWING TOOLS

Excel provides many tools for you to draw and format shapes and text boxes in your worksheet.

Draw Shapes

1. Click the 🖾 button on the Standard toolbar to open the Drawing toolbar.

2. Select the shape you want to draw in your worksheet: **Line** ◻, **Arrow** ◼, **Rectangle** ▢, or **Oval** ⬭.

3. Click in the worksheet and drag the crosshatch pointer to the desired shape size.

Add Shape Color

1. Click on the shape you want to color in your worksheet.

2. Click the appropriate button to select how you want to apply the color: **Fill Color** 🎨 and **Line Color** 🖌. Click the desired color.

Alter Shape Style

1. Click on the shape to which you want to apply a style in your worksheet.

2. Click the appropriate button to select how you want to apply the style: **Line Style** ☰, **Dash Style** ▦, **Arrow Style** ▤, **Shadow** ◨, **3-D** ◪. Choose the desired style.

Insert AutoShapes

1. Click [AutoShapes ▾] and select the particular shape you want to add to your worksheet from the submenus.

2. Click in the worksheet and drag the crosshatch pointer to the desired shape size.

Rotate Shapes

1. Click on the shape you want to rotate in your worksheet.

2. Click the ⟳ button on the Drawing toolbar.

3. Click the rotate pointer on one of the object's *round* rotate handles and drag the object to the desired rotation.

Add a Text Box

1. Click the ▤ button on the Drawing toolbar, or choose **Insert, Textbox**.

2. Click in the worksheet and drag the crosshatch pointer to the desired shape size.

3. Click the ⊠ button and select the color for the font and type the information you want in the text box.

See Also AutoShape, Clip Art, Objects, Word Art

EMAIL

You can send the contents of the current Excel workbook as the substance of the email message or as an attachment to the email message.

Send Workbook As an Email

1. Click the **Email** ⊞ button on the Standard toolbar and, if prompted, choose the option to **Send the current sheet as the message body** and click ⊏ OK ⊐ to continue.

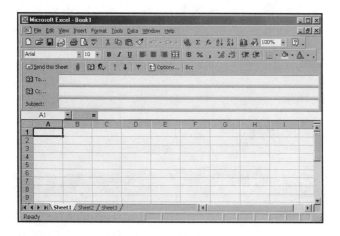

2. Type the **To, Cc,** and any changes to the **Subject** line (this defaults to the filename) and any other changes in the message.

3. Click ⊞Send this Sheet⊐ and it is sent.

TIP

Click the **Email** ⊞ button again if you decide not to send the workbook as an email and want to return to the workbook.

Send Workbook As an Email Attachment

1. Choose **File, Send To, Mail Recipient (as Attachment)**. This opens an email message and inserts the current workbook as an attachment.

2. Type the **To, Cc,** and any changes to the **Subject** line (this defaults to the filename) and any other changes in the document.

3. Click  and it is sent.

See Also Web Pages

EMBEDDED OBJECTS
see Links   pg 80; Objects   pg 90

ERROR MESSAGES

In Excel, a formula calculates a value based on the values in other cells of the workbook. Excel displays the result of a formula in a cell as a value. When the result is an error, there are some basic steps you can take to correct it.

Fix the #### Error

1. When a cell contains ####, the column is not wide enough to display the data. The data and any formulas in the cell are intact, just not visible in the space provided.

2. Click on the column border and drag it to increase the size of the column width. The error disappears.

Fix the #DIV/0! Error

1. When a cell contains **#DIV/0!**, the formula is trying to divide a number by 0 or an empty cell.

2. Correct your formula to eliminate the zero or empty cell reference. Press (↵Enter) to make the error disappear.

Fix the #NAME? Error

1. When a cell contains **#NAME?**, the formula contains incorrectly spelled cell or function names.

2. Correct your formula to eliminate the incorrect reference. Press (↵Enter) to make the error disappear.

Fix the #VALUE! Error

1. When a cell contains **#VALUE!**, the formula contains nonnumeric data or cell or function names that cannot be used in the calculation.

2. Correct your formula to eliminate the incorrect reference. Press (↵Enter) to make the error disappear.

Recognize the #REF! Error

1. When a cell contains **#REF!**, the formula contains a reference to a cell that isn't valid. Frequently, this means you deleted a referenced cell.

2. Undoing your action can sometimes be the best option, as well as reviewing the cells involved in the formula.

Recognize Circular References

1. A circular reference results when one of the cells you are referencing in your calculation is the cell in which you want the calculation to appear. This might actually be your desired result, for example if you are using scientific and engineering formulas requiring circular references.

2. Choose one of the following in the Microsoft Excel message box: [Cancel], if you intend to create a circular reference, the [OK] button if you want to edit and correct your formula, or the [Help] button if you want

Excel to help you create and understand circular references.

See Also Spelling

EXIT EXCEL

When you no longer want to work in Excel, exit the application and return to the Windows desktop.

Quick Tip		
Feature	*Button*	*Keyboard Shortcut*
Exit	☒	Alt + F4

Exit Excel

1. Click the ☒ button in the upper-right corner of the application window. You will be asked whether you want to save your work.

2. Click ⬛Yes to save your work (refer to **Save Workbooks** if you have problems saving your work); click ⬛No to close any unsaved changes; and click ⬛Cancel to return to working in the document.

See Also Save Workbooks, Start Excel

EXPENSE STATEMENT

You can use Excel's Expense Statement spreadsheet solution to create your own expanse statement. This can be convenient when you don't want to create one from scratch.

Use Excel's Expense Statement Spreadsheet Solutions

1. Choose **File, New** to open the New dialog box.

2. Click the **Spreadsheet Solutions** tab.

3. Double-click the **Expense Statement** icon.

4. Click [Enable Macros] and begin altering the sample expense statement to how you want it to appear for your purposes.

5. Choose **File, Save As,** which will open a Template File - Save to Database message box.

6. Choose from the **What would you like to do?** options:

   - **Create a new record:** Create a new expense statement to be saved in your database.

   - **Continue without updating:** Create a new expense statement without saving it in a database.

   - **Update the existing record:** You will only see this option if you are resaving the file and want to update the expense statements in your database.

7. Click [OK] in the Template File - Save to Database dialog box.

8. Type a **File name** in the Save As dialog box and click [Save] to save the expense statement as a workbook file.

See Also Invoice, Purchase Order

FAX

Faxing a worksheet is as easy as printing a worksheet. Keep in mind that to fax a worksheet you must have fax software installed on your computer and an outgoing phone line.

Send a Worksheet As a Fax

1. Choose **File, Print** to open the Print dialog box.

2. Select **Microsoft Fax** (or whatever fax software you have installed) from the **Printer Name** drop-down list box.

3. Select the print to fax options (**Print range, Copies,** and **Print What**).

F

54

4. Click [OK] to send the fax. Depending on your fax software, you will be prompted to enter the phone number to which you want to fax, recipient name, and a fax cover letter, if necessary.

See Also Help, Print

FILES

Instead of copying and pasting data and pictures into worksheets, you can insert an entire file.

Insert a File

1. Choose **Insert, Object; Create from File** tab to open the Object dialog box.

2. Select the **File name** and choose from the following options:

   - **No option:** Inserts the file contents without a link, you can open the application you used to create the file and edit the information.

   - **Link to file:** Inserts the file contents with a link, any changes you make to the original source file will be reflected in your workbook.

   - **Display as icon:** Inserts the file as an icon representing the contents of the file. You can also select the **Link to file** along with it for changes to the original source file to be reflected in the icon in your workbook.

3. Click [OK]. The text and objects from the selected file are inserted directly into and are now part of your worksheet.

TIP

You can click [Browse...] in the Object dialog box if you need to open the Browse dialog box and locate the file you want to insert into your workbook.

Insert a Picture File

1. Choose **Insert, Picture, From File** to open the Insert Picture dialog box.

2. Locate the **File name** and click [Insert]. The picture from the selected file is inserted directly into and is now part of your worksheet.

TIP

You can resize and work with the picture file the same way you resize objects, see the section on "Objects" for more information.

See Also Objects, Hyperlinks

FILTER DATA

In a large, columnar list of data, you might not want to see each and every row. Instead, you might want to work with just a set of rows. When you want to work with a subset of rows, you can filter the data. All the rows remain in the worksheet, but only those meeting the criteria you select are visible.

Filter Data

1. Select the column titles for the data you want to filter.

2. Choose **Data, Filter, AutoFilter** to toggle between filtering columns and add drop-down arrows to each column title.

3. Click the arrow next to the column you want to use for the filtering criteria.

4. Select the filtering criteria you want to match. You can select a particular value:

   - **All:** Display all the records in the list.
   - **Top 10:** Use the **Show** options in the Top 10 AutoFilter dialog box to display the **Top** or **Bottom 1** through **500 Items**; or display the **Top** or **Bottom Percentage**.

- **Custom:** Use the **Show rows where** options in the Custom AutoFilter dialog box to display records that may meet a set of criteria.

Excel displays only those records that meet the selected criteria. You can tell the last has been filtered because the filter arrow is a different color.

Perform an Advanced Filter

1. Set up a criteria range that holds the specifications used in your advanced filter. This criteria range must contain at least two rows: the first row must contain the field names from the list and the remaining rows must contain the filtering criteria.

2. Choose **Data, Filter, Advanced Filter** to open the Advanced Filter dialog box.

3. Click the **List range** collapse dialog box ![button] button and select the range of the list you want to filter.

4. Click the **List range** expand dialog box ![button] button to return to the Advanced Filter dialog box.

5. Click the **Criteria range** collapse dialog box ![button] button and select the range of the criteria for what you are wanting to filter on.

6. Click the **Criteria range** expand dialog box ![button] button to return to the Advanced Filter dialog box.

7. Click ![OK] to perform the advanced filter and review the filtered list in the worksheet.

TIP

To see the entire list again, choose **Data, Filter, Show All**.

See Also Data Lists, Sort Data

FIND DATA

You can use Excel's Find feature to locate data, text, characters, formatting, or even special characters.

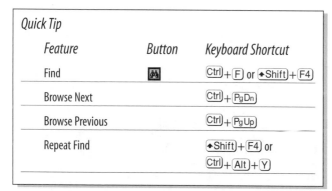

Quick Tip		
Feature	*Button*	*Keyboard Shortcut*
Find	🔍	Ctrl+F or ◆Shift+F4
Browse Next		Ctrl+PgDn
Browse Previous		Ctrl+PgUp
Repeat Find		◆Shift+F4 or Ctrl+Alt+Y

Find Regular Data

1. Choose **Edit, Find** to open the Find dialog box.

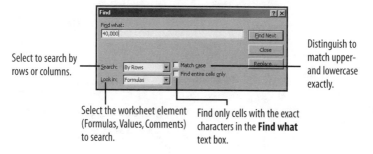

Select to search by rows or columns.

Distinguish to match upper- and lowercase exactly.

Select the worksheet element (Formulas, Values, Comments) to search.

Find only cells with the exact characters in the **Find what** text box.

2. Type the text you want to locate in the **Find what** text box.

3. Click [Find Next] to move to each occurrence within the worksheet. If there aren't any to be found, Excel notifies you that it has finished searching the worksheet and that the item wasn't found.

See Also Browse, Replace Text

FIND FILES

Excel enables you to set very specific criteria for locating files of which you cannot remember the filename. You can perform all types of file searches, not only searches for Excel workbooks.

Find a File

1. Click the **Open** 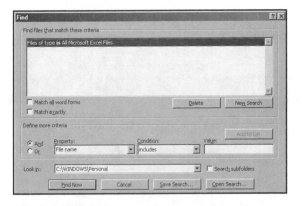 button on the Standard toolbar to open the Open dialog box.

2. Click the **Tools** drop-down list at the top right of the dialog box and choose **Find**.

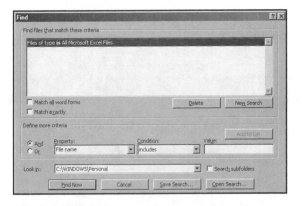

3. Click the **Look in** drop-down list box to look in a particular drive or folder. In the **Find files that match these criteria** section, you may choose to either look for a filename that will **Match all word forms** or **Match exactly**.

4. Click the **Property, Condition,** and **Value** drop-down list boxes in the **Define more criteria** section to match a property (**File name, Comment, Author,** and so on) with a conditional value (**includes, begins with, ends with**).

5. Click [Find Now] to begin the search. If you cannot find the file, click [New Search] and try again.

See Also Open Worksheets, Save Worksheets

FLIP ROWS AND COLUMNS

Flipping rows and columns (transposing) is a special copy feature you might need to use if you want to change the layout of your worksheet. This can be convenient when you need to change the way your data is displayed for user readability.

Transpose Data

1. Select the range of cells you want to transpose. Click the **Copy** 🖻 button.

2. Click the first cell in which you want to paste the copied range.

3. Choose **Edit**, **Paste Special** to open the Paste Special dialog box.

4. Select the **Transpose** check box and click the ⬚ OK ⬚ button. The range is transposed (or flipped) when pasted.

> **TIP**
>
> Note that you cannot transpose a range of cells onto the original range selection. You must first transpose the range and then move the range to its original location.

See Also Columns, Paste, Rows

FONTS

To draw attention to important data in a worksheet, you can change the text font options.

Quick Tip	
Feature	*Keyboard Shortcut*
Font	Ctrl + ⬆Shift + F
Font Size	Ctrl + ⬆Shift + P

Change Existing Fonts

1. Select the cells where you want to draw attention to or place your cursor where you plan to type your text.

2. Click the **Font** drop-down list box on the Formatting toolbar and select the desired font.

3. Click the **Font Size** drop-down list box on the Formatting toolbar and select the desired font size.

4. Click the **Font Color** drop-down list box on the Formatting toolbar and select the desired font color.

TIP

New in Office 2000 is the ability to see a sample of a font in the **Font** drop-down list box. You can see what the font looks like before you apply it to your cells. This helps you choose the right font faster.

Add Font Effects to Data

1. Select the cells to which you want to add a font effect.

2. Choose **Format, Cells; Font** tab.

Sets the underline to none, single, double, or single/double accounting.

Draws a line through the selected data.

Formats the selected data as superscript (powers).

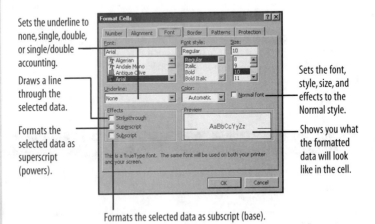

Sets the font, style, size, and effects to the Normal style.

Shows you what the formatted data will look like in the cell.

Formats the selected data as subscript (base).

3. Select from the various types of **Effects**.

4. Click the [OK] button to accept changes and return to the worksheet.

TIP

You can also select a font color (or another option) before you begin typing. All of the data in a cell will then be that color.

Change the Default Font

1. Choose **Format, Cells; Font** tab.

2. Select the **Font, Font Size**, and **Size** that you want to be the default font in your worksheet.

3. Click [OK] and the font will become the default font for only that current worksheet.

TIP

To format only a portion of a cell's data, select only that portion and then change the font.

See Also Format, Highlight Text, Styles, Text

FORMAT

To draw attention to important data in a worksheet, you can format the data with any combination of bold, italic, and underline.

Quick Tip

Feature	Button	Keyboard Shortcut
Bold	**B**	Ctrl + B
Italic	*I*	Ctrl + I
Underline	U	Ctrl + U
Double Underline		Ctrl + ⬆Shift + D
Strikethrough		Ctrl + 5

Format Bold, Italic, and Underline

1. Select the cells or text you want to format.

2. Click the ⬛ button to add bold; *I* to add italic; and ⬛ to add underline to your data.

See Also Cells, Font, Format Painter

FORMAT PAINTER

You can use the Format Painter to copy the formatting from a selected object or cell and apply it to a different object or cells you select.

Copy Formats

1. Select the cells or objects containing the format you want to duplicate.
2. Click the ⬛ button on the Standard toolbar.
3. Select the cells or objects to which you want to reformat; it formats automatically.

Copy Formats to Multiple Locations

1. Select the cells or objects containing the format you want to duplicate.
2. Double-click the ⬛ button on the Standard toolbar.
3. Select each particular set of cells, or object to automatically reformat.
4. Click the ⬛ button again when you are finished applying the format.

See Also Cells, Copy and Cut, Paste

FORMULAS

In Excel, a formula calculates a value based on the values in other cells of the workbook (whether it be a single cell, range of cells, or cells you have given a range name). Excel displays the result of a formula in a cell as a numeric value. Sometimes you don't want to use AutoSum because you have specific cell references on which you want to perform calculations. In this instance, you can simply type the desired formula directly into the cell.

Quick Tip

Feature	Keyboard Shortcut
Start a Formula	$=$
Cancel Formula Bar Entry	Esc
Edit Active Cell	F2
Paste Name in Formula	F3
Paste Function Into Formula	Shift + F3
Define Name	Ctrl + F3
Calculate All Sheets	F9
Calculate Active Worksheet	Shift + F9
Insert AutoSum Formula	Alt + $=$
Enter Date	Ctrl + ;
Enter Time	Ctrl + Shift + :
Switch Cell Value/Formula	Ctrl + '
Display AutoComplete List	Alt + PgDn

D
E
F

Enter a Formula

1. Click the cell where you want the result of a formula to appear.

2. Type the equals sign , the cell numbers, and the calculation for Excel to perform on the cells. The formula is displayed in the Formula bar. If you start to enter a formula and then decide you don't want to use it, you can skip entering the formula by pressing Esc.

TIP

Excel first performs any calculations within parentheses: (1+2)=3. Then it performs multiplication or division calculations from left to right: (12+24)/(3×2)=6. Finally, it performs any addition or subtraction from left to right: (12+24)/(3×2)-5=1.

Edit a Formula

1. Click the cell with the formula to make it the active cell. Notice that the formula is displayed in the Formula bar.

2. Click the **Edit Formula** ▣ button and type or delete any changes to your formula. You can use the arrow keys to move within the cell data or the Del or ⬅Backspace keys to delete data.

3. Click ⬚ OK ⬚. The changes are made and the result appears in the cell.

TIP

In addition to using the Formula bar to edit your formulas, you can simply press F2 and edit your formula just like you would regular text or data.

Copy a Formula

1. Click the cell that contains the formula you want to copy.

2. Click the **Copy** ▣ button on the Standard toolbar.

3. Click and drag the mouse pointer over all the cells where you want to paste the function. A line will surround the cell you are copying.

4. Press ⬅Enter to paste the formula into each of the specified cells.

Define a Cell or Range Name

1. Select the cell or range of cells you want to name in order to use the range name in a formula.

2. Choose **Insert, Name, Define** to open the Define Name dialog box, which displays the range coordinates and suggests a name.

3. Type the range name you want to use and click ⬚ OK ⬚. Excel names the range. When the range is selected, it appears in the **Name** box to the left of the Formula bar.

> **TIP**
>
> Begin a cell or range name with a letter or underscore. You can include upper- and lowercase letters and you can include up to 255 characters. Don't use a range name that looks like a cell reference and don't include spaces.

Use a Range Name in a Formula

1. Click the cell where you want to enter a formula.
2. Type the formula to find a total using a named range and press ⏎Enter. Notice that the formula is displayed in the Formula bar.

> **TIP**
>
> If you forget the name of a range while you are typing a formula choose **Insert, Name, Paste**. The Paste Name dialog box will allow you to select the desired range name and place it automatically in the formula.

See Also AutoCalculate, AutoSum, Cells, Functions

FREEZE PANES

Many times your worksheet will be large enough that you cannot view all the data onscreen at the same time. In addition, if you have added row or column titles, and you scroll down or to the right, some of the titles will be too far to the top or left of the worksheet for you to see. To help, you can freeze the heading rows and columns so they're always visible.

Freeze Rows and Columns

1. Click in the cell to the right of and below the area you want to freeze and choose **Window, Freeze Panes**.
2. Move through the worksheet (use the scrollbars) and notice that the rows and columns you selected are frozen so you can reference data with the appropriate titles.

3. Choose **Window, Unfreeze Panes** to remove the freezing of columns and rows.

See Also Cells, Columns, Rows, Split Windows, Workspace

FUNCTIONS

Functions are abbreviated formulas that perform a specific operation on a group of values. Excel provides over 250 functions to help you with tasks ranging from determining loan payments to calculating investment returns.

Insert a Function

1. Click the cell in which the result of the function will appear.

2. Click the **Paste Function** 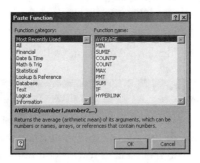 button on the Standard toolbar to open the Paste Function dialog box.

3. Select the **Function Category** and scroll through the function names.

4. Click on the **Function name** to review the function description at the bottom of the dialog box. The following are a few commonly used functions:

   - **AVERAGE:** Returns the arguments average.

   - **MIN:** Returns the smallest argument number.

   - **SUMIF:** Adds the cells specified by a given condition or criteria.

   - **COUNTIF:** Counts the cells specified by a given condition or criteria.

- **COUNT:** Returns the number of cells that contain number arguments.
- **MAX:** Returns the largest argument number.
- **PMT:** Calculates a loan payment based on constant payments and interest rates.
- **SUM:** Adds the numbers in a range of cells.
- **IF:** Returns different values if a condition is TRUE or FALSE.
- **HYPERLINK:** Creates a shortcut link to a stored document or the Internet.

5. Click [OK] after you have selected the function you want. Excel selects the obvious range of cells.

6. Type the cell range or range name and press ⏎Enter. Or, click the Collapse dialog box 🔝 button, select the cell range in the worksheet itself, and click the Expand dialog box 🔲 button. The calculated result appears in the active cell and the function is displayed in the Formula bar.

See Also AutoCalculate, AutoSum, Cells, Formulas

GET EXTERNAL DATA

You can retrieve external data from database files into Excel. You might want to use this information to perform calculations, run reports, or create new worksheets when the database is large, shared, or in a format that Excel cannot read.

Use an External Database

1. Load the MS Query add-in in your Excel application (see the **Add-Ins** section for more information); choose **Tools, Add-Ins**, select the **MS Query Add-In** option, and click [OK] to return to the worksheet and use MS Query.

2. Choose **Data, Get External Data, New Database Query** to open the Choose Data Source dialog box.

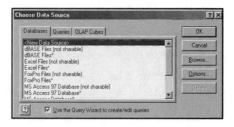

3. Select the type of database you want to retrieve data from and click [OK]. Make sure she **Use the Query Wizard to create/edit queries** option is selected by default.

4. Locate the actual database in the Select Database dialog box and click [OK]; the Query Wizard appears.

5. Select the **Columns in your query** from the **Available tables and columns** list boxes. You can choose an entire table or click the ⊞ sign to select columns within a table.

6. Click the [>] button to move the selection of the columns or tables to your query. Then click [Next >].

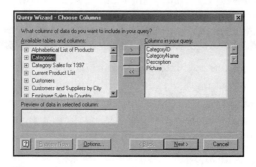

7. Select any columns that you want to filter in the **Column to filter list** and select the criteria in the **Only include rows where** column drop-down list. Then click [Next >].

8. Select the **Sort by** drop-down list if you want to sort the criteria you have selected and choose **Ascending** or **Descending** order. Then click [Next >].

9. Click the **Return Data to Microsoft Excel** option and click [Finish] to accept your query options and return to the Excel workbook. You can also click the **Save Query** button to keep the query for future use.

10. Select whether you want to place the results of the query in the current worksheet or in a new worksheet and click [OK]. The results will appear in Excel.

See Also Filter Data, Sort Data

GOAL SEEK

Excel enables you to make a formula return a desired value. You can actually adjust the value in a specified cell until a formula that is dependent on that cell reaches a target value. For example, you can use this feature to find out how many sales you will need to make in a desired month to meet your quarterly sales expectations.

Use Goal Seek

1. Click in the cell that contains the formula for the type of calculation you desire.

2. Choose **Tools, Goal Seek** to open the Goal Seek dialog box. The current cell is listed in the **Set cell** list box, but you can alter that if necessary.

3. Type the desired value you seek in the **To value** text box.

4. Type in the cell that you must change to reach the goal in the **By changing cell** list box.

5. Click [OK] to perform the Goal Seek. A Goal Seek Status dialog box will appear if the goal is attainable (click [OK] to accept the goal seek change or click

the [Cancel] button to return the cells to their previous data). If not, you will see a message box telling you that your information is not valid. You can either change the current **To** value in the Goal Seek dialog box, increase the number of **Maximum iterations** in the **Calculation** tab of the Options dialog box (choose **Tools, Options; Calculation** tab), or review your formula logic to make sure the formula cells aren't dependent on the changing cell.

See Also Formulas, Functions, Scenarios

GO TO

The Go To command enables you to move quickly to any cell in a worksheet or workbook. In addition, you can go to specific *special* cells that meet a conditional criteria.

Quick Tip	
Feature	Keyboard Shortcut
Go To	Ctrl+G or F5

Use Go To

1. Choose **Edit, Go To** to open the Go To dialog box.
2. Type the cell reference and click [OK]. Excel moves to the selected cell.

Go To Special Selections

1. Select a range of cells that you want to search through; otherwise Excel will review the active area of the worksheet (where you have entered data and formulas).
2. Choose **Edit, Go To** to open the Go To dialog box.
3. Click [Special...] to open the **Go To Special** dialog box.

4. Choose the **Select** option for the item you are looking for.

5. Click the [OK] button and Excel moves to the selected cell. If there isn't a cell that matches the criteria selection, Excel will notify you with a message box that no cells were found.

See Also Find Data, Move Data, Replace Data

GROUPING
see Outline   pg 96

HEADER AND FOOTER

Headers and footers can appear at the top and bottom of printed pages of Excel worksheets. Headers and footers can display the filename, date and time printed, worksheet name, page number, and more.

Insert Header and Footer

1. Choose **View, Header and Footer; Header and Footer** tab.

2. Click the **Header** drop-down list box to see the various header options; or click [Custom Header...] to create your own header. When you create a custom header, Excel saves the format so you can select it in the future from the **Header** drop-down list.

3. Click the option you want to be in the left, center, and right section of the header.

4. Click [Custom Footer...] if you want to create your own footer; or click the Footer drop-down list box and select from the options. When you create a custom footer, Excel saves the format so you can select it in the future from the **Footer** drop-down list.

5. Press [Tab↹] to move through the left, center, and right sections.

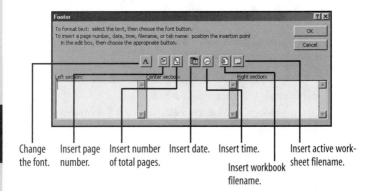

Change the font.   Insert page number.   Insert number of total pages.   Insert date.   Insert time.   Insert workbook filename.   Insert active worksheet filename.

6. Click the appropriate button to automatically insert information into the footer section or type your text into the appropriate section.

7. Click [OK] to accept the footer text.

8. Click [OK] to accept the header and footer text.

9. Click the [🔍] button on the Standard toolbar to see how your worksheet previews.

TIP

You can alter your header and footer while in the Print Preview window by selecting [Setup...] on the Print Preview toolbar and clicking the Header/Footer tab.

See Also Page Setup, Print, Print Preview, Views

HELP

There are a couple different ways you can get help in Excel 2000. The **Help Contents** option is similar to using the table of contents in a book. The **Answer Wizard** option behaves similar to the Office Assistant where you ask questions and it searches for related topics. In the **Help Index** option, you type the word or phrase you want to find, and then you can view a list of all matching topics. What's This? Help offers a ScreenTip command with concise information about the command's function.

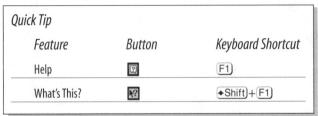

Quick Tip

Feature	*Button*	*Keyboard Shortcut*
Help	[?]	F1
What's This?	[?]	◆Shift + F1

Get Contents Help

1. Press F1; **Contents** tab.
2. Click on the **+** of a topic to list all the subtopics.
3. Click on a subtopic to see the information displayed in the description area.

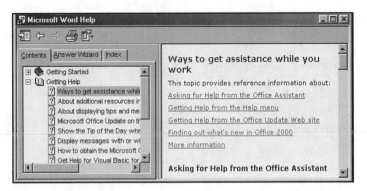

4. Click the ☒ button to exit Help.

> **TIP**
>
> If a word or phrase is underlined, it means that you can display a pop-up definition for the term. Point to the term and click the mouse button. A definition appears.

Get Answer Wizard Help

1. Press (F1); **Answer Wizard** tab.
2. Type in your question.

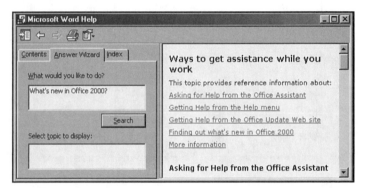

3. Click [Search] and select the topic from the frame on the right that you want to display.
4. Click the ☒ button to exit Help.

Get Index Help

1. Press (F1); **Index** tab.
2. Type in a keyword and then click [Search].

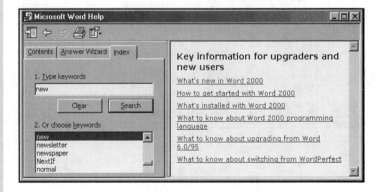

3. Select the topic you want in the description area.

4. Click the ⊠ button to exit Help.

Print Help Topics

1. Select the Help item you want to print.

2. Click the 🖨 button on the toolbar.

Use What's This?

1. Choose **Help, What's This?** and the mouse pointer becomes a question mark pointer.

2. Click the command or object you want explained and read the What's This? pop-up.

3. Click anywhere in your workspace, or press the (Esc), (Alt), or (F10) keys to clear the pop-up information.

See Also Detect and Repair, Office Assistant, Office on the Web

HIGHLIGHT
see Patterns   pg 103

HYPERLINKS

When you click on a hyperlink, the worksheet appears to *jump* to the related location. A hyperlink is an active link to a file, location, or element you want to move to.

Quick Tip

Feature	*Button*	*Keyboard Shortcut*
Insert Hyperlink	🔗	(Ctrl)+(K)

Type a URL Hyperlink Into a Worksheet

1. Click the cell in the worksheet where you want to add the hyperlink.

2. Type the URL into your worksheet and press (↵Enter), the address will automatically become a hyperlink.

3. Move the mouse pointer over the hyperlink and the location of the hyperlink's destination will display in a ScreenTip.

TIP

In addition to linking to another document or workbook, you can paste cells as a hyperlink. This will enable you to click on the items in the pasted area and immediately be hyperlinked to your original workbook that contains the cells. Choose **Edit**, **Paste Hyperlink** in the document into which you are pasting.

Insert a Hyperlink

1. Select the cells that you want to convert to a hyperlink.
2. Click the **Insert Hyperlink** 🖼 button on the Standard toolbar to open the Insert Hyperlink dialog box.
3. Type the link into the **Type the file or Web page name** text box, select a link from the **Recent Files**, **Browsed Pages**, or **Inserted Links** list.

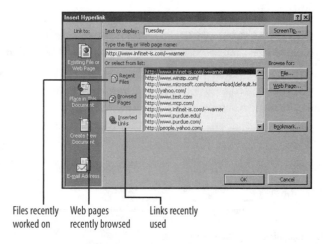

Files recently   Web pages   Links recently
worked on   recently browsed   used

4. Click [ok] to accept changes and return to the worksheet.

See Also Objects, Text, Save Worksheets, Web Pages

IF

The IF function is one of Excel's many built-in formulas for performing a specialized calculation on the data in your worksheet. It returns one value if TRUE and another value if FALSE in a range of cells.

Enter an IF Function

1. Click the cell where you want the result of the function to appear.

2. Click the ☒ button on the Standard toolbar to open the Paste Function dialog box.

3. Double-click the **IF** option in the **Most Recently Used Function Category**, **Function Name** list box. Excel opens an **IF** function box.

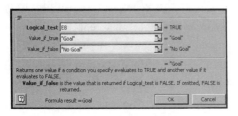

4. Type the **Logical_test** data (for example, C4>C5) and press (Tab↹).

5. Type the **Value_if_true** to be displayed in the cell if the logical test is **TRUE** and press (Tab↹).

6. Type the **Value_if_false** to be displayed in the cell if the logical test is **FALSE**.

7. Click [OK] to accept your values. The result appears in the active cell and the function is displayed in the Formula bar.

See Also AVERAGE, COUNTIF, MAX, MIN, SUMIF

ITALICS
see Format   pg 61

INVOICE

You can use Excel's Invoice spreadsheet solutions to create your own invoice. This can be convenient when you don't want to create one from scratch.

Use Excel's Invoice Spreadsheet Solutions

1. Choose **File, New** to open the New dialog box.

2. Click the **Spreadsheet Solutions** tab.

3. Double-click the **Invoice** icon.

4. Click [Enable Macros] and begin altering the sample invoice to how you want it to appear for your purposes.

5. Choose **File, Save As**, which will open a Template File - Save to Database message box.

6. Choose from the **What would you like to do?** options:

   - **Create a new record:** Create a new expense statement to be saved in your database.

   - **Continue without updating:** Create a new expense statement without saving it in a database.

   - **Update the existing record:** You will only see this option if you are resaving the file and want to update the expense statements in your database.

7. Click [OK] in the Template File - Save to Database dialog box.

8. Type a **File name** in the Save As dialog box and click
   [🖫 Save] to save the expense statement as a workbook
   file.

See Also Expense Statement, Purchase Order

JUSTIFICATION

see Alignment   pg 4

LANDSCAPE

see Page Setup   pg 99

LINKS

Objects and data in Excel can be linked to other sources and files. You can easily update, open, or change the links to refer to different objects, files, and data.

Update a Link

1. Open the file that contains a linked object.

2. Choose **Edit, Links** to open the Links dialog box. Any linked Source files will be listed with the file and folder location.

3. Click the **Update Now** button to update the link and click the [OK] button to return to the worksheet.

Open a Link Source

1. Open the file that contains a linked object.

2. Choose **Edit, Links** to open the Links dialog box. Any linked **Source files** will be listed with the file and folder location.

3. Click the **Open Source** button to open the linked file.

4. Make any changes to the workbook file and click the **Close** ⊠ button to return to the file containing the linked object; any changes appear automatically.

Change a Link Source

1. Open the file that contains a linked object.

2. Choose **Edit, Links** to open the Links dialog box. Any linked **Source files** are listed with the file and folder location.

3. Click the **Change Source** button to change the linked filename in the Change Links dialog box.

4. Click the **Places bar** option for the location of the file you want to open.

5. Click the **Look in** drop-down list box to help locate the correct file or drive. You can also click the 🖻 button to move through folders.

6. Double-click the file you want to link to and Excel updates the **Source file** in the Links dialog box. Click the [OK] button to return to the worksheet with the updated link.

See Also Objects, Paste

MACROS

You can create a macro to accomplish just about any task. With the macro recording option, you can record your actions, and then these actions will be performed for you whenever you run the macro.

Quick Tip		
Feature	*Button*	*Keyboard Shortcut*
Macro	▶	Alt + F8
Stop Recording	■	
Relative Reference	🖾	

Create a Macro

1. Choose **Tools, Macro, Record New Macro** to open the Record Macro dialog box.

2. Type a name in the **Macro name** text box.

3. Click the [OK] button. The Stop Recording macro toolbar appears with the **Stop Recording** ■ and **Relative Reference** 🖾 buttons.

4. Perform any tasks that you want the macro to record and click the **Stop Recording** ▣ button when finished.

TIP

The **Relative References** ▦ button determines whether the Macro recorder uses relative references or absolute references (the default) to worksheet cells.

Run a Macro

1. Press (Alt)+(F8) to open the Macros dialog box.

2. Double-click on the **Macro name** to run the macro.

TIP

You can learn how to add buttons to your toolbars in the **Toolbars** section. Macros can also be added to your toolbars to make it easier to launch them. For example, follow along the steps of adding a button to your toolbar, but choose **Macros** from the **Categories** list. Then choose the specific macro from the **Commands** list.

Modify or Delete a Macro

1. Choose **Tools, Macro, Macros** to open the Macro dialog box.

2. Click on the **Macro name** and click the appropriate button to perform the modification you desire:

   - Edit—This opens the Visual Basic Editor to the macro code. Make any changes and click the **Close** ☒ button to return to your document.

   - Delete—This asks you if you want to delete the macro. Click the Yes button to delete the macro. Click the Close button to return to your document.

See Also Find Text, Replace Text

MARGINS
see Page Setup   pg 99; Print Preview   pg 111

MAX

The maximum function is one of Excel's many built-in formulas for performing a specialized calculation on the data in your worksheet. It finds the largest number in a range of data.

Find a Maximum

1. Click the cell where you want the result of the function to appear.

2. Click the 𝑓x button on the Standard toolbar to open the Paste Function dialog box.

3. Double-click the **MAX** option in the **Most Recently Used Function Category**, **Function Name** list box. Excel automatically inserts what it considers the most likely range to be averaged based on the cell that you have chosen for your results.

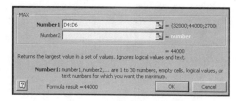

4. Accept this range or type the cell range or range name you want and click the ⌐ OK ⌐ button. The result appears in the active cell and the function is displayed in the Formula bar.

TIP

If Excel doesn't automatically select the cells you want, you can select them yourself by clicking in the first cell, holding down ⟨⬆Shift⟩, and clicking in the last cell.

See Also AVERAGE, COUNTIF, MIN, SUMIF

MENUS

The menu bar is just below the title bar and the available commands vary depending on what you are doing in Excel.

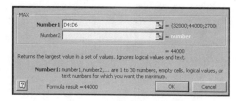

You select commands on the menu to perform operations. Excel 2000 now has a *personalized* menu option, which displays only those commands relevant to what you are doing in the document at that time.

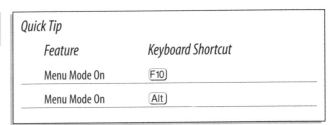

Quick Tip	
Feature	*Keyboard Shortcut*
Menu Mode On	F10
Menu Mode On	Alt

Use Personalized Menus

1. Click on the menu category that you want to open.
2. Click on the [　　　　　　　　 ⫶ 　　　　　　　] button to show all the commands available.

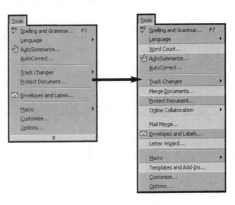

3. Click the command on the menu you want and the menu closes automatically.

Use Regular Menus

1. Click on the menu category that you want to open (**File**, **Edit**, and so on).
2. Click the command on the menu you want and the menu closes automatically.

Close a Menu Without Choosing a Command

1. Click on the menu category that you want to open.

2. Click elsewhere on the desktop or press (Esc), (Alt), or (F10) to close the menu.

Turn Personalized Menus On/Off

1. Choose **Tools, Customize; Options** tab.

2. Select the **Menus show recently used commands first** option if you want to turn the personalized menus on. Deselect the option to turn them off.

3. Click the [Close] button to accept changes and return to the document.

See Also Dialog Boxes, Toolbars

MERGE WORKBOOKS

You can combine multiple workbooks into one main workbook as well as merge comments and changes.

Merge Workbooks

1. Open the main workbook into which you want to merge other workbooks and or comments/changes. Make sure both workbooks are shared and have different filenames (see the sections **Share Workbooks** and **Save** for more information).

2. Choose **Tools, Merge Workbooks** to open the Select File to Merge into Current Workbook dialog box.

3. Double-click on the document you want to merge into the current document. If asked, click the [OK] button or the [Cancel] button if there are any untracked changes.

See Also Comments, Save, Share Workbooks, Track Changes

MIN

The minimum function is one of Excel's many built-in formulas for performing a specialized calculation on the data in your worksheet. It will find the smallest number in a range of data.

Find a Minimum

1. Click the cell where you want the result of the function to appear.

2. Click the ▣ button on the Standard toolbar to open the Paste Function dialog box.

3. Double-click the **MIN** option in the **Most Recently Used Function Category**, **Function Name** list box. Excel automatically inserts what it considers the most likely range to be averaged based on the cell that you have chosen for your results.

4. Accept this range or type the cell range or range name you want and press ⏎Enter). The result appears in the active cell and the function is displayed in the Formula bar.

TIP

If Excel doesn't automatically select the cells you want, you can select them yourself by clicking in the first cell, holding down ⬆Shift), and clicking in the last cell.

See Also AVERAGE, COUNTIF, MAX, SUMIF

MOVE CELLS

You can reorganize cells in an Excel worksheet by moving items as you work. This method can be faster than cutting and pasting text.

Move Cells to a New Location

1. Select the cells you want to move.

2. Press and hold down the left mouse button on the border of the selected cells, and drag the pointer to the new location.

3. Release the mouse button to drop the cells in the new location.

See Also Copy and Cut, Objects, Paste

#NAME?
see Error Messages   pg 50

NAME
see Formulas   pg 62

NEW WORKBOOK

Excel presents a new blank workbook each time you start the application. You can create another new workbook at any time. In addition, Excel provides templates that can help you create different types of new workbooks.

Quick Tip		
Feature	*Button*	*Keyboard Shortcut*
New Workbook	🗋	Ctrl + N
Insert New Worksheet		⬆Shift + F11 or Alt + ⬆Shift + F1

Create a New Workbook

Click the 🗋 button on the Standard toolbar and Excel opens a new workbook.

Use a New Workbook Spreadsheet Solution

1. Choose **File**, **New** to open the New dialog box. Select the tab that corresponds with what you want to create.

2. Double-click either the worksheet to begin inserting the new text or the spreadsheet solution template, filling in information as necessary.

> **TIP**
>
> The default filename for each new workbook (Book1, Book2, Book3, and so on) automatically increases sequentially. If you exit and start Excel again, the numbers begin at 1 again.

See Also Open Workbook, Worksheets

NUMBERS

You can apply different styles to cells, depending on the type of data the cells contain. Using styles affects the way cells display data but does not limit the type of data you can enter.

Quick Tip		
Feature	*Button*	*Keyboard Shortcut*
Format Style		Alt + '
Format Cells		Ctrl + 1
General Number Format		Ctrl + Shift + ~
Currency Format	💲	Ctrl + Shift + $
Percentage Format	%	Ctrl + Shift + %
Exponential Format		Ctrl + Shift + ^
Date Format		Ctrl + Shift + #
Time Format		Ctrl + Shift + @
Number Format		Ctrl + Shift + !

Numeric Data Options

1. Select the cells you want to format.

2. Click the **Increase Decimal** 🔢 or **Decrease Decimal** 🔢 button on the Formatting toolbar to increase or decrease the number of decimal places.

3. Click the **Comma Style** 🔢 button on the Formatting toolbar to apply commas to numbers.

4. Click the **Percent Style** 🔲 button on the Formatting toolbar to apply percentages to numbers.

5. Click the **Currency Style** 🔲 button on the Formatting toolbar to apply the currency style to numbers.

TIP

You can immediately make a number a textual cell entry by typing an apostrophe (') before you type in the number, this tells Excel that the number is text.

Change Cell Number Format

1. Select the cells you want to format.

2. Choose **Format, Cells; Number** tab.

Display decimal places, negative numbers, and currency symbols.

Display decimal places and negative numbers.

No specific number format.

Display decimal places and currency symbols.

Display date types.

Display time types.

Display percentages with decimal places.

Display types of fractions.

Display decimal places.

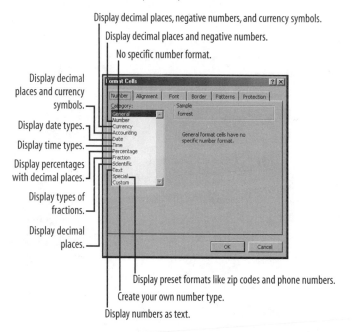

Display preset formats like zip codes and phone numbers.

Create your own number type.

Display numbers as text.

3. Click the **Category** option and click the [OK] button to accept the changes and return to the worksheet.

TIP

To quickly format numbers back to the general format, choose **Edit, Clear, Formats**. Excel clears all the formatting and returns the numbers to their original general format.

See Also Cells, Fonts, Styles

OBJECTS

An Excel object can be any of numerous types of elements that you can add to your worksheet: file, art, chart, worksheet, photo, movie, text clip, and so on.

Insert a New Object

1. Choose **Insert, Object; Create New** tab.
2. Click on the **Object type** from the list box. Click the [OK] button to accept changes and return to the worksheet.
3. Click directly on the object and make any changes to it using the associated toolbar.

Insert an Object File

1. Choose **Insert, Object; Create from File** tab.
2. Type in the filename or click the [Browse...] button to select the file from a specific location.
3. Select the **Link to file** option if you want the object to be linked to this worksheet and the source file. This means that any changes you make in the source file are reflected in your worksheet.
4. Click the [OK] button to accept changes and return to the worksheet.

Resize Objects

1. Click once directly on an object to make a handle appear on each side and corner of the object.
2. Move the mouse pointer over one of the handles; click and hold the handle when the pointer becomes a two-headed arrow.

M
N
O

3. Drag the handle to the desired size. If you drag from the corner handles, the height and width increase or decrease proportionately. Drag the handle on top to increase height and the handle on the side to increase width.

4. Click elsewhere in the worksheet to deselect the object.

Move Objects

1. Click once directly on an object to make a handle appear on each side and corner of the object.

2. Move the mouse pointer over the object, click and hold the pointer when the pointer appears with a gray box below it. Drag the object to the new location and drop the object.

TIP

To select multiple objects, click the first object, and then press and hold down the Shift key and click on the second object. Continue doing this until all the objects you want are selected.

Delete Objects

1. Click once directly on an object to make a handle appear on each side and corner of the object.

2. Press Del to remove the object from the worksheet.

TIP

If you link an object in your worksheet, you can quickly edit or open the source file by double-clicking the object. You can also copy, cut, and paste an object to a different location.

See Also Clip Art, Drawing Tools, Excel Worksheets

OFFICE ASSISTANT

The Office Assistant is the default way to search for help on a particular topic and find shortcuts in Excel worksheets using normal, plain English questions. It helps you find instructions and tips for getting your work done more easily.

Quick Tip

Feature	Button	Keyboard Shortcut
Help	🔲	F1

Show and Hide the Office Assistant

1. Choose **Help, Show the Office Assistant**.
2. Choose **Help, Hide the Office Assistant**.

Ask the Office Assistant Questions

1. Click on the **Assistant** character if it is onscreen; otherwise, click the **Microsoft Excel Help** 🔲 button on the Standard toolbar.
2. Type in the question or term for which you want information and click the ⬜ button.
3. Click the bullet next to the information you want and then select the topic you want Microsoft Office to reference.
4. Click the **Close** ❌ button in the upper-right corner of the Help window to close the help window.
5. Right-click the **Assistant** and click **Hide** from the shortcut menu. This simply hides the assistant from the screen, see the section **Turn the Assistant Off** to make it go away completely.

Change the Assistant

1. Right-click the **Assistant** and click **Choose Assistant** from the shortcut menu.
2. Scroll through the different Assistant options using the ⬜ and ⬜ buttons in the Gallery page of the Office Assistant dialog box.
3. Click the ⬜ button when you finish selecting an Assistant.

Turn the Assistant Off

1. Right-click the **Assistant** and click **Options** from the shortcut menu.

2. Click to deselect the **Use the Office Assistant** option and click the [OK] button.

See Also Detect and Repair, Help, Office on the Web, What's This?

OFFICE ON THE WEB

Microsoft Office on the Web takes you to the Microsoft Office Web site and provides you with access to download free stuff, product news, updates, frequently asked questions, online support, and many other ways to get information.

Microsoft Office Update Web Site

1. Choose **Help, Office on the Web**.
2. Peruse the Microsoft Office Web Site with your Web browser.
3. Click the **Close** ☒ button when you want to return to the document.

See Also Detect and Repair, Help, Office Assistant, What's This?

OPEN WORKBOOK

Each time you want to work with a workbook, you need to open it using the Open dialog box.

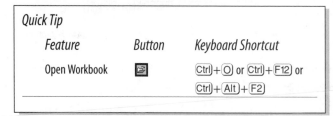

Quick Tip

Feature	Button	Keyboard Shortcut
Open Workbook	🖻	Ctrl+O or Ctrl+F12 or Ctrl+Alt+F2

Open a Workbook

1. Click the **Open** 🖻 button on the Standard toolbar to open the Open dialog box listing the saved Excel workbooks.

Files in the My Documents folder (sometimes called the Personal folder).

Most recent 80 files.

Places bar

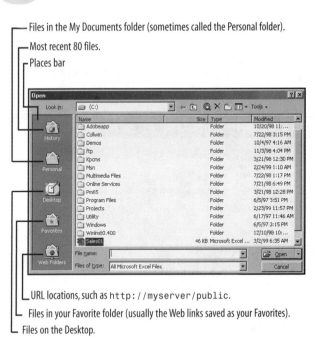

URL locations, such as http://myserver/public.

Files in your Favorite folder (usually the Web links saved as your Favorites).

Files on the Desktop.

2. Click the **Places bar** option for the location of the file you want to open.

3. Click the **Look in** drop-down list box to help locate the correct file or drive. You can also click the 🖻 button to move through folders.

4. Double-click the file you want to open and Excel opens the workbook.

TIP

Click the **File** menu to display a list of recently opened and saved files at the bottom of the **File** menu.

Open Files of Different Type

1. Click the **Open** 🖻 button on the Standard toolbar to open the Open dialog box listing the saved Excel workbooks.

2. Click the **Files of type** drop-down list box and select the file type. The Open dialog box displays only files that are of the type you selected. Then, locate the folder that contains the file you want to open.

3. Double-click the file you want to open and Excel opens the workbook. If the file cannot be opened because there is a compatibility error, Excel alerts you of this with a message box.

TIP

To preview the document before you open it, click the **Views** 📰 drop-down button on the Open dialog box toolbar and select **Preview**. The document will display in the Preview Pane on the right side of the Open dialog box. The Open dialog box will stay in Preview Pane view until you alter the view again or exit Word.

See Also New Workbook, Save Workbook

ORGANIZATION CHART

You can insert an Organization Chart object into your worksheet quickly and easily. In addition, you can make changes to your chart and save them in a worksheet.

Insert an Organization Chart

1. Choose **Insert, Picture, Organization Chart** to open the Microsoft Organization Chart window.

`[toolbar] 🗋 🗁 🖫 🖨 🔍 ✌ | 🖵 🗈 🖺 ✍ | 🔊 ▾ ⏣ ▾ | 🖳 Σ 🎓 ½ ¾ | 📖 🚚 100% ▾ 🔃 .`

2. Click in the workspace and type the appropriate titles, names, and comments for each **Manager, Subordinate, Assistant**, and **Coworker**.

3. Use the Organization Chart's Standard toolbar to add any additional items to the organization chart.

4. Choose **File, Exit and Return to Worksheet**. Excel prompts you to save any changes to the chart if you haven't already. Click the `Yes` button to save changes and close the chart. Click the `No` button to close the chart without saving changes. Click the `Cancel` button to return to working in your chart without closing it.

> **TIP**
>
> To make any changes to the chart, double-click on the chart in your worksheet and save changes as necessary.

See Also AutoShapes, Clip Art, Drawing Tools, Objects

ORIENTATION
see Page Setup   pg 99

OUTLINE

Using Excel you can select a range of cells and organize the data based on formulas and the direction of referenced information. An outline helps you display hierarchical information in different levels of detail.

Quick Tip	
Feature	*Keyboard Shortcut*
Group Rows or Columns	Alt + Shift + →
Ungroup Rows or Columns	Alt + Shift + ←
Display/Hide Outline Symbols	Ctrl + 8
Hide Selected Rows	Ctrl + 9
Unhide Selected Rows	Ctrl + Shift + (
Hide Selected Columns	Ctrl + 0
Unhide Selected Columns	Ctrl + Shift +)

Create an Outline Automatically

1. Click the cell pointer anywhere in the range of the data you want to outline.

2. Choose **Data, Group and Outline, Auto Outline**. Excel determines where the natural breaks are in the formula ranges.

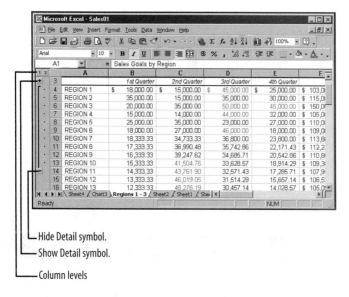

— Hide Detail symbol.
— Show Detail symbol.
—— Column levels

Create an Outline Manually

1. Select an entire row(s) that you want to include in the outline group you are going to create. Make sure you don't include a row that contains any summary formulas.

2. Choose **Data, Group and Outline, Group**. Excel assigns that group an outline level for the rows it contains.

3. Repeat steps 1 and 2 for each group you want to create.

TIP

You can create groups of groups to create outlines with multiple levels. Make sure that you start with the innermost groupings and work your way out in the worksheet data.

Work with an Outline

1. Click the - ▤ to collapse the level of an outline; click the + ⊞ to expand the level of an outline.

2. Click the number symbols [1], [2], and so on to display a level that corresponds to the number. The [1] collapses the outline completely, the largest [*number*] expands the outline completely.

M
N
O

> **TIP**
>
> You can Press Ctrl+8 to toggle between hiding and showing the outline symbols; this is convenient when you want another user to see only the information displayed, and not to know that some information is hidden in the outline.

Remove an Outline

Choose **Data, Group and Outline, Clear Outline** to remove the outline and display all the data in the worksheet.

See Also Views, Workspace

PAGE BREAK

When in Print Preview or Page Break Preview, you can see dashed lines that indicate where the worksheet will break when printed. If you don't want to alter the worksheet to fit, you can simply add a manual page break indicating where you want the worksheet to break the columns or rows for printing.

Insert a Vertical Page Break

1. Click the cell in **Column A** where you want to begin a new page vertically.

2. Choose **Insert, Page Break** to apply the page break.

3. Click the **Print Preview** 🔍 button to review the new page break.

> **TIP**
>
> If you select a cell outside Column A or Row 1, Excel will insert a horizontal and vertical page break.

Insert a Horizontal Page Break

1. Click the cell in **Row 1** where you want to begin a new page horizontally.

2. Choose **Insert, Page Break** to apply the page break.

3. Click the **Print Preview** 🔍 button to review the new page break.

See Also Page Setup, Print, Print Preview

PAGE SETUP

You can adjust the page orientation, scaling, paper size, and margins for worksheets. In addition, you can set options to print your work in numerous ways.

Set Margins

1. Choose **File, Page Setup**; **Margins** tab.

2. Type in or use the spin box controls to set the **Top, Bottom, Left, Right** margins, and **Header** and **Footer** sizes from the document edge.

3. Click the ▭ OK ▭ button to accept changes and return to the worksheet.

TIP

You can click and drag any of the margin or column guides to see how you can alter your worksheet when in Print Preview.

Change from Portrait to Landscape

1. Choose **File, Page Setup**; **Page** tab.

2. Select either **Portrait** or **Landscape** for the **Orientation**. Click the ▭ OK ▭ button to accept changes and return to the worksheet.

Select the Paper Size

1. Choose **File, Page Setup**; **Page** tab.

2. Select the **Paper size** from the drop-down list box. Click the ▭ OK ▭ button to accept changes and return to the worksheet.

Select the Page Scale

1. Choose **File, Page Setup**; **Page** tab.

2. Select the **Adjust to % normal size** percentage you want the page to size to or adjust the spin box controls to **Fit to** the number of **page(s) wide by** number of **tall**.

3. Click the [OK] button to accept changes and return to the worksheet.

Print Cell Comments

1. Choose **File, Page Setup; Sheet** tab.

2. Click the **Comments** drop-down list and select either to print the comments **At end of sheet** or **As displayed on sheet**.

Center Printed Output

1. Choose **File, Page Setup; Margins** tab.

2. Click either **Horizontally** or **Vertically** in the **Center on page** option.

3. Click the [OK] button to accept changes and return to the worksheet.

Print Draft Quality

1. Choose **File, Page Setup; Page** tab.

2. Click the **Print quality** drop-down list and select from the dots per inch (dpi) options. The lower the number the faster the print, but also the lower the quality and the fewer the items that Excel prints in your worksheet (for example, charts don't print at 75 dpi).

3. Click the [OK] button to accept changes and return to the worksheet.

Choose Beginning Page Number

1. Choose **File, Page Setup; Page** tab.

2. Type a number into the **First page number** list box if the first page needs to start with something other than the automatic number.

3. Click the [OK] button to accept changes and return to the worksheet.

See Also Alignment, Columns, Print, Print Area Print Preview

PASTE

You can share information within and between worksheets in Excel (and other Windows applications) by pasting cells and objects. You can now paste up to 12 different items from the Clipboard at a time. The Clipboard is where items are stored after you copy or cut them.

Quick Tip		
Feature	*Button*	*Keyboard Shortcut*
Paste	🖻	Ctrl + V or ⇧Shift + Insert
Paste Function Into Formula		⇧Shift + F3

Paste Text or Objects

1. Place the cursor in the location where you want to paste the cells or object. You must have already cut or copied cells or an object for the **Paste** 🖻 button to be active.

2. Click the **Paste** 🖻 button on the Standard toolbar.

Paste Multiple Items

1. Choose **View, Toolbars, Clipboard** to open the Clipboard toolbar. You must have already cut or copied cells or an object for there to be any items on the Clipboard.

2. Place the cursor in the location where you want to paste a cut or copied item.

P
Q
R

Paste all items in the worksheet.

Copy an item to the clipboard.

Delete all items from the clipboard.

Paste an item into the worksheet.

3. As you move the mouse pointer over the items on the Clipboard toolbar a ScreenTip displays what is contained in each clip (unless the clip is extensive, then only part of it is displayed).

4. Move the mouse pointer to where you want to insert the text or object. Click the clip that you want to paste. When finished, click the **Close** ⊠ button to close the Clipboard toolbar, or choose **View**, **Toolbars**, **Clipboard** to toggle the toolbar closed.

Paste Special

1. Click in the cell where you want to paste the cells or object. You must have already cut or copied cells or an object.

2. Choose **Edit**, **Paste Special** to open the Paste Special dialog box.

3. Select the **Paste** and **Operation** options for how you want to paste the copied cells.

4. Click the [Paste Link] button to create a shortcut link to the source file or cells (any changes you make to the source file or cells are automatically reflected in your worksheet).

5. Click the [OK] button to accept changes and return to the worksheet.

Paste Data As a Picture

1. Click in the cell where you want to paste a picture of the data you copied. You must have already cut or copied cells or an object for the **Paste** 📖 button to be active.

2. Press (◆Shift) and choose **Edit**, **Paste Picture** to paste the copied cells as a picture. You can delete or resize the picture just like you would any other object.

See Also Copy and Cut, Hyperlink, Move Cells, Objects, Replace Data

PATTERNS

You can apply colors and patterns to the background of selected cells.

Apply Cell Shading

1. Select the cells you want to shade.

2. Choose **Format, Cells; Patterns** tab.

3. Select a **Color** and click the **Pattern** drop-down list box to apply a pattern to the background of the cell.

4. Click the [OK] button to accept changes and return to the worksheet.

> **TIP**
>
> Be sure a shading or color pattern doesn't interfere with the readability of data. The data still needs to be legible; you might need to make the text bold or choose a complementary text color. If you're going to print the worksheet to a non-color printer, the color you choose will print gray. The darker the gray, the less readable the data. Yellow generally prints to a pleasing light gray that doesn't compete with the data.

> **TIP**
>
> You can also click a color from the **Fill Color** drop-down palette on the Formatting toolbar to apply only a cell color.

See Also Borders, Cells, Fonts

PIVOTTABLES AND PIVOTCHARTS

PivotTables are interactive reports that summarize and analyze Excel worksheet data or an external database. You can alter your data analysis without creating a new report each time. A PivotTable cross-tabulates data in columns and rows and enables you to filter and sort the display data as well as expand the field details.

Quick Tip

Feature	*Keyboard Shortcut*
Group Selected PivotTable Items	(Alt)+(⬆Shift)+(→)
Ungroup Selected PivotTable Items	(Alt)+(⬆Shift)+(←)

Create a PivotTable and a PivotChart Report

1. Select a cell in the worksheet table that you want to serve as the foundation for the PivotTable (usually column headers).

2. Choose **Data, PivotTable and PivotChart Report** to open the PivotTable and PivotChart Wizard.

3. Select the **Microsoft Excel list or database** option for the data that you want to analyze and whether you want to create a **PivotTable** or **PivotChart** report, then choose the [Next >] button. Excel automatically selects the range of cells for the pivot table, but allows you to change it in the second step of the wizard.

4. Verify or reselect the range of cells (there must be more than one row selected), then choose the [Next >] button.

5. Select where you want to place the PivotTable, either in a **New worksheet** or the **Existing worksheet**. Also select from the [Layout...] or [Options...] buttons to format or alter your settings, then choose the [Finish] button.

Lay out the report (OLAP) in a dialog box or alter page field settings (non-OLAP) instead of in a worksheet.

Alter formatting, layout, memory, and external data options.

Select the cells in the existing worksheet for the PivotTable placement.

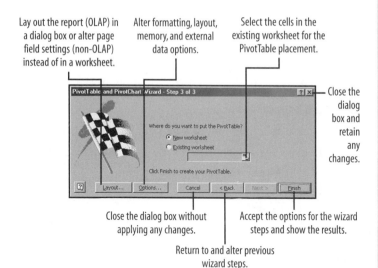

Close the dialog box and retain any changes.

Close the dialog box without applying any changes.

Accept the options for the wizard steps and show the results.

Return to and alter previous wizard steps.

6. Click the particular field you want to summarize on the PivotTable toolbar and drag it into the **DATA** area. Click and drag the fields you want on the **PAGE** and in **ROWS** and **COLUMNS**. You can move these fields back and forth if you select one in error.

Drop page fields here.   Drop column fields here.

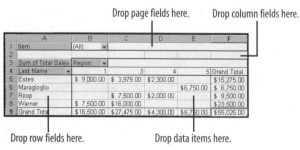

Drop row fields here.   Drop data items here.

7. Click the **Chart Wizard** button on the PivotTable toolbar to create a new chart sheet based on the PivotTable you just created. You can move the fields around in the chart using the PivotTable toolbar. If you already closed the toolbar, choose **View, Toolbars, PivotTable** to display it.

Group PivotTable Items

1. Select the cells to be grouped.
2. Choose **Data, Group and Outline, Group** to create a new field consisting of the selected items.

Group Items Automatically

1. Select only one item in a field.
2. Choose **Data, Group and Outline, Group** to open the Group dialog box.
3. Select the grouping options in the **By** list box.
4. Click the ⬛ᴏᴋ⬛ button and Excel automatically creates the groups.

Insert a New Field Into a PivotTable

1. Click the cell pointer anywhere in the PivotTable.
2. Choose **View, Toolbars, PivotTable** to open the PivotTable toolbar.
3. Click on a field and drag it to the desired location in the PivotTable diagram.

Remove a Field from a PivotTable

Click on a field and drag it off the PivotTable diagram.

Work with a PivotTable

1. Click and drag the PivotTable fields to modify the pivot table's structure.
2. Choose **Data, Refresh Data** (or click the **Refresh Data** ▣ button) to refresh the data in the PivotTable as often as you want.

See Also Charts, Data Lists

PMT

The PMT function is one of Excel's many built-in formulas for performing a specialized calculation on the data in your worksheet. It calculates the payment for a loan, based on constant payments and a constant interest rate.

Calculate a Payment

1. Click the cell where you want the result of the function to appear.

2. Click the **Paste Function** 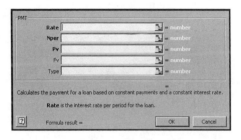 button on the Standard toolbar to open the Paste Function dialog box.

3. Double-click the **PMT** option in the **Most Recently Used Function Category**, **Function Name** list box. Excel opens the PMT function box.

PMT		
Rate		= number
Nper		= number
Pv		= number
Fv		= number
Type		= number

Calculates the payment for a loan based on constant payments and a constant interest rate.

Rate is the interest rate per period for the loan.

Formula result = | OK | Cancel |

4. Type the **Rate** (interest rate), **Nper** (total number of payments), and **Pv** (present value). Both **Fv** (future value—cash balance to attain after the last payment is made) and **Type** (payment at the beginning of the period) are optional.

5. Click the [OK] button to accept the values. The result appears in the active cell and the function is displayed in the Formula bar.

> **TIP**
>
> If Excel doesn't automatically select the cells you want, you can select them yourself by clicking in the first cell, holding down (⬆Shift), and clicking in the last cell of the range.

See Also COUNTIF, MAX, MIN, SUMIF

PORTRAIT
see Page Setup   pg 99

PRINT

Excel makes it easy to print a worksheet and enables you to select the printer and worksheet settings.

Quick Tip

Feature	Button	Keyboard Shortcut
Print		Ctrl + P or
		Ctrl + ◆Shift + F12

Set Print Area

1. Select the cells you want to print.
2. Choose **File, Print Area, Set Print Area**; repeat this if you need to reset the area. You can select **Clear Print Area** if you need to remove the set print area.

Print Noncontiguous Ranges

1. Choose **File, Print Area, Clear Print Area** to clear the print area, if one is set.
2. Press Ctrl while you select each of the cell ranges you want to print.
3. Choose **File, Print** to open the Print dialog box.
4. Click the **Selection** option in the **Print what** area and click the ⬚ ok ⬚ button to send the print job.

Print Current Worksheet Defaults

Click the **Print** 🖨 button on the standard toolbar; the worksheet prints according to the settings in your page setup.

TIP

Click the ⬚ Cancel ⬚ button on the Print dialog box to cancel the print. In addition, if you already sent the workbook to the printer, click the ⬚ Cancel ⬚ button on the Printing message box that appears as soon as you click the ⬚ ok ⬚ button.

Change Print Defaults

1. Open a new blank worksheet and alter the print settings as described in this section and the Page Setup section.

2. Choose **File, Save As** to open the Save As dialog box.

3. Click the **Save as type** drop-down list option and select **Template**.

4. Type **Book.xlt** in the **Filename** drop-down list box and click the 🖫 Save button to save the worksheet. This template is used as the new default custom print settings.

Enter Print Options

1. Choose **File, Print** to open the Print dialog box.

Print all
pages in the ——
worksheet.

Print the
page range
specified in ——
the spin
boxes.

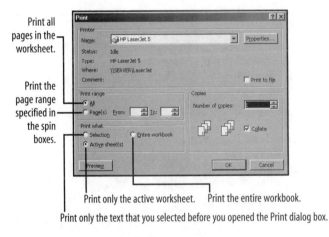

Print only the active worksheet.   Print the entire workbook.
Print only the text that you selected before you opened the Print dialog box.

2. Select the **Page range** that you want as your print job.

3. Select the **Number of copies** you want printed, whether you want Excel to **Collate** a multiple page worksheet.

4. Click the [OK] button to send the print job to the printer.

Print Column or Row Titles

1. Choose **File, Page Setup; Sheet** tab.

2. Click the **Collapse Dialog Box** 🔢 button in the **Rows to repeat at top** text box and drag directly in your worksheet to select the rows you want to repeat on multiple printed pages.

3. Click the **Expand Dialog Box** 🔲 button to return to the full Page Setup dialog box.

4. Click the **Collapse Dialog Box** 🔢 button in the **Columns to repeat at left** text box and drag directly in your worksheet to select the columns you want to repeat on multiple printed pages.

5. Click the **Expand Dialog Box** 🔲 button to return to the full Page Setup dialog box.

6. Click the [OK] button to accept changes and return to the worksheet.

TIP

You cannot assign repeating titles while you are in the Print Preview window; to do this, you must be in the worksheet view and select **Page Setup** from the **File** menu.

Print Gridlines and Sheet Options

1. Choose **File, Page Setup; Sheet** tab.

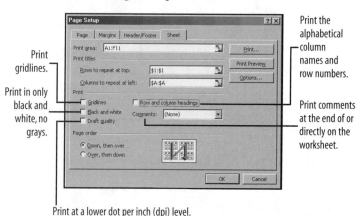

Print gridlines.

Print in only black and white, no grays.

Print the alphabetical column names and row numbers.

Print comments at the end of or directly on the worksheet.

Print at a lower dot per inch (dpi) level.

2. Select from the various print **Sheet** options. Click the  button to accept changes and return to the worksheet.

Choose a Different Printer

1. Choose **File**, **Print** to open the Print dialog box.
2. Click the **Name** drop-down list box and select the printer you want to print to.

See Also Page Setup, Print Preview

PRINT PREVIEW

Print Preview enables you to see worksheet pages onscreen as they will appear printed on paper, displaying page numbers, headers, footers, fonts, orientation, columns and rows, gridlines, and margins.

Quick Tip

Feature	*Button*
Print Preview	

Preview a Worksheet

1. Click the **Print Preview** button on the Standard toolbar.
2. Click directly on the previewed worksheet to increase the magnification.
3. Click directly on the previewed worksheet again and the magnification returns to the original percentage.
4. Click the Close button on the Print Preview toolbar to return to the worksheet.

TIP

Click the Margins button on the Print Preview toolbar again to toggle the margins on and off. This will allow you to select each page or column indicator and alter the margins and column widths.

> **TIP**
>
> To view other pages in the worksheet, click the `Next` or `Previous`
> buttons on the Print Preview toolbar. To print the worksheet,
> click the **Print** button.

See Also Page Setup, Print, Views, Workspace

PRINT LAYOUT VIEW
see Workspace   pg 144

PROPERTIES

Details about a file that help identify it—author's name,
document title, topic, keywords—are known as file properties. Use file properties to help organize your files or display
file information. This can be convenient information to
have saved if you need to search for a particular file.

Add Worksheet Summary Information

1. Choose **File, Properties; Summary** tab.
2. Type the information about your document that you
   want to save.
3. Click the `OK` button to return to the document.

Read Worksheet Statistics

1. Choose **File, Properties; Statistics** tab.
2. Review the statistical information about your document.
3. Click the `OK` button to return to the document.

See Also Files

PROTECT WORKBOOKS

When you share files with other users, you might find it
useful to protect your workbooks. You can protect your
workbooks by restricting access to the workbook and preventing changes being made within each particular workbook.

Protect Sheet

1. Choose **Tools, Protection, Protect Sheet**.

2. Select the options of what to **Protect worksheet for**.
   Contents prevents changes to cells and chart items.
   Objects prevents editing, moving, deleting, or resizing
   of objects in worksheets and chart sheets. **Scenarios**
   prevents changes to worksheet scenario definitions (set
   of values for input cells).

3. Type a password in the **Password (optional)** option and
   press ⏎Enter. This means that any other user needs to
   enter this password to open this workbook.

4. Type the same password in the Confirm Password dialog
   box and press ⏎Enter. (If asked to save the workbook,
   choose ▢ OK ▢.)

Protect Workbook

1. Choose **Tools, Protection, Protect Workbook**.

2. Select the options of what to **Protect workbook for**.
   Structure protects worksheets from being added,
   deleted, moved, hidden, unhidden, or renamed.
   Windows protects the workbook windows from begin
   moved, closed, resized, hidden, or unhidden.

3. Type a password in the **Password (optional)** option and
   press ⏎Enter. This means that any other user needs to
   enter this password to open this workbook.

4. Type the same password in the Confirm Password dialog
   box and press ⏎Enter. (If asked to save the workbook,
   choose ▢ OK ▢.)

Protect Shared Workbook

1. Choose **Tools, Protection, Protect and Share
   Workbook**.

2. Select that you want to **Protect workbook for Sharing with track changes.** You are able to share the workbook, but any changes that others make are tracked and only you can accept them.

3. Type a password in the **Password (optional)** option and press ↵Enter). This means that any other user needs to enter this password to open this workbook.

4. Type the same password in the Confirm Password dialog box and press ↵Enter). (If asked to save the workbook, choose ⬚OK⬚.)

CAUTION

Don't forget the password you assign to your workbooks. If you forget or misplace the password, you will not be able to access the workbook again. Choose a password you can remember but that others can't guess. Avoid names of pets or family. The hardest passwords to guess are at least five characters long and contain at least one symbol character, such as $, %, &, or @.

See Also Comments, Share Workbooks, Track Changes

PURCHASE ORDER

You can use Excel's Purchase Order spreadsheet solution to create your own purchase order. This is convenient when you don't want to create one from scratch.

Use Excel's Purchase Order Spreadsheet Solutions

1. Choose **File, New** to open the New dialog box.

2. Click the **Spreadsheet Solutions** tab.

3. Double-click the **Purchase Order** icon.

4. Click the ⬚Enable Macros⬚ button and begin altering the sample purchase order to how you want it to appear for your purposes.

5. Choose **File, Save As**, which will open a Template File-Save to Database dialog box.

6. Choose from the **What would you like to do?** options:

- Create a new record: Create a new purchase order to be saved in your database.
- Continue without updating: Create a new purchase order without saving it in a database.
- Update the existing record: You will only see this option if you are resaving the file and want to update the purchase orders in your database.

7. Click the [ok] button in the Template File - Save to Database dialog box.

8. Type a **File name** in the Save As dialog box and click the [Save] button to save the purchase order as a workbook file.

See Also Expense Statement, Invoice

REDO
see Undo   pg 138

#REF!
see Error Messages   pg 50

REPLACE DATA

You can quickly replace numbers, text, data formats, and special characters in Excel.

Quick Tip	
Feature	*Keyboard Shortcut*
Replace	Ctrl + H

Search and Replace Data

1. Choose **Edit, Replace** to open the Find and Replace dialog box.

2. Type the text you want to change in the **Find What** text box. Any text from a previous search will still be in the dialog box; unless you have exited Excel.

3. Click in the **Replace With** text box (or press Tab⇄) and type the text you want to replace it with.

4. Select from the Search options and click the appropriate action button.

P
Q
R

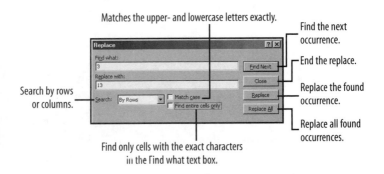

Matches the upper- and lowercase letters exactly.

Find the next occurrence.

End the replace.

Search by rows or columns.

Replace the found occurrence.

Replace all found occurrences.

Find only cells with the exact characters in the Find what text box.

See Also Copy and Cut, Find Data, Move Data, Paste, Redo, and Undo

RIGHT ALIGN
see Alignment   pg 4

ROWS

Rows are a horizontal set of cells in a worksheet labeled with numbers.

Quick Tip	
Feature	*Keyboard Shortcut*
Hide Rows	Ctrl + 9
Unhide Rows	Ctrl + ⬆Shift + (

Insert Rows

1. Select a row or cell where you want to add a row.

2. Choose **Insert, Rows** to insert the row above the original cell or row selection. Or, right-click the row and choose **Insert** from the shortcut menu.

Delete Rows

1. Click the row heading of the row you want to delete.

2. Choose **Edit, Delete** to delete the row. Or, right-click the row and choose **Delete** from the shortcut menu.

Hide Rows

Click and drag the bottom border of a row past the top (row). Or, select the row and choose **Format, Row, Hide**.

Unhide Rows

Select the row above and below the row you want to unhide and choose **Format, Row, Unhide**.

> **TIP**
>
> Hidden elements don't print when you print the worksheet.

Format Rows

1. Select a cell in the row you want to format.
2. Choose **Format, Row** and select the appropriate option from the submenu.

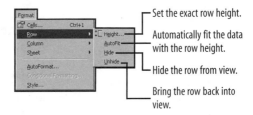

— Set the exact row height.

Automatically fit the data with the row height.

— Hide the row from view.

Bring the row back into view.

> **TIP**
>
> To make multiple rows the same height, click the mouse and drag over all the row headers you want resized. Then resize one of the rows. Each row becomes that size.

> **TIP**
>
> To automatically make a row fit the height of the tallest cell, choose **Format, Row, AutoFit**.

See Also Cells, Columns, Freezing Panes, Workspace

SAVE WORKBOOKS

Save the workbook you are working in to store it for later use. It is good practice to frequently save your workbooks as you work in them. In addition, you can set Excel to save your work automatically.

> *Quick Tip*
>
> | Feature | Button | Keyboard Shortcut |
> |---------|--------|-------------------|
> | Save | 🔲 | Ctrl+S or ⬆Shift+F12 or Alt+⬆Shift+F2 |
> | Save As | | F12 or Alt+F2 |

Save a Worksheet

1. Click the **Save** 🔲 button on the Standard toolbar and the workbook saves any recent changes. If you haven't saved the workbook yet, the Save As dialog box appears.

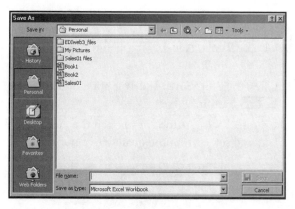

2. Click the **Places bar** option for the location of the file you want to save.

3. Click the **Save in** drop-down list box to help locate the correct folder or drive. You can also click the **Up One Level** 🔲 button to move through folders.

4. Type the filename and click the 🔲 Save button.

Save As a Different Name

1. Choose **File, Save As** to open the Save As dialog box.

2. Click the **Places bar** button for the location of the file you want to save.

3. Click the **Save in** drop-down list box to help locate the correct folder or drive. You can also click the **Up One Level** 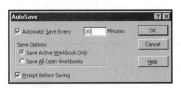 button to move through folders.

4. Type the new filename and click the **Save** button.

Save as a Different File Type

1. Choose **File, Save As** to open the Save As dialog box.

2. Click the **Places bar** button for the location of the file you want to save. Click the **Save in** drop-down list box to help locate the correct folder or drive. You can also click the **Up One Level** button to move through folders.

3. Click the **Save as type** drop-down list box and select the desired file type. Type the filename and click the **Save** button.

Save Work Automatically

1. Choose **Tools, Add-Ins** to open the Add-Ins dialog box.

2. Click the **AutoSave Add-In** option and click the **OK** button.

3. Choose **Tools, AutoSave** to open the AutoSave dialog box and select from the available options.

4. Click the **OK** button to accept changes and return to your document.

TIP

To stop automatically saving your work when in Excel workbooks, repeat step 3 and deselect the **Automatic Save Every** option and click the **OK** button. To remove AutoSave Add-In, repeat steps 1 and 2 (but deselect AutoSave Add-In instead).

See Also Close Workbooks, Open Workbooks, Worksheets, Workspace

SCENARIOS

A scenario is a set of values for input cells. These scenarios can be used to perform what-if analyses to observe the effects on one or more dependent formulas. You can assign a name to a scenario, and you can display them using the scenario manager.

Create a Named Scenario

1. Create a workbook with cells that change based upon the results of one or more formulas.

2. Choose **Tools, Scenarios** to open the Scenario Manager dialog box.

3. Click the [Add] button to add a scenario.

4. Type in a scenario name and enter the cell references to the **Changing cells**. If any of the changing cells contain a formula, Excel will alert you that to continue, the cell formula will be changed to a constant value.

5. Repeat steps 3 and 4 for each scenario you would like to add.

6. Click on the particular scenario in the Scenario Manager dialog box and click the [Show] button to see the scenario displayed in the worksheet.

S
T
U

Create a Scenario Summary Report

1. Create a workbook with cells that change based upon the results of one or more formulas.

2. Choose **Tools, Scenarios** to open the Scenario Manager dialog box.

3. Create scenarios using the previous **Create a Named Scenario** Section.

4. Click the [Summary...] button and select the **Scenario Summary Report type** option to create a report on the scenario options.

5. Select the **Result cells** and click the [OK] button to display the scenario summary report.

Merge Scenarios

1. Create a workbook with cells that change based upon the results of one or more formulas.

2. Choose **Tools, Scenarios** to open the Scenario Manager dialog box.

3. Create scenarios in multiple worksheets of a workbook using the previously mentioned "Create a Named Scenario" section.

4. Click the [Merge...] button to merge the selected scenarios from a worksheet into an open workbook in the Merge Scenarios dialog box.

5. Select the **Book** and **Sheet** that contain the scenarios that you want to merge and click the [OK] button.

6. Click on the particular dated merge scenario in the Scenario Manager dialog box and click the [Show] button to see the merged scenario displayed in the worksheet.

See Also Formulas, Functions, Goal Seek

SCREENTIPS
see Toolbars   pg 135

SEARCH
see Find Data   pg 57

SHADING

see Patterns   pg 103

SHARE WORKBOOKS

You can share workbooks either by restricting access to the worksheet or by preventing changes from being made within each particular worksheet.

Set File Share Options

1. Choose **Tools, Share Workbook** to open the Share Workbook dialog box.

2. Select whether you want to **Allow changes by more than one user at the same time**. This saves the workbook as a shared workbook.

3. Click the [OK] button to accept changes and return to the worksheet.

See Also Comments, Protect Workbooks, Track Changes

SPELLING

You can check spelling in Excel 2000 quickly and easily. Of course, you should always review your workbooks, but it never hurts to have a little help.

Quick Tip		
Feature	*Button*	*Keyboard Shortcut*
Spelling	⚏	F7
Next Misspelling		Alt + F7

Check Spelling

1. Click the **Spelling** ⚏ button on the Standard toolbar. The Spelling dialog box opens, displaying the first spelling error it finds.

2. Click the appropriate spelling option in the **Suggestions** list box; if one doesn't work, type the correction directly in the **Change to** text box.

3. Click the appropriate button to make the selected **Suggestions** change, whether to add, ignore, change, and so on.

A spelling that shouldn't be altered and should not be flagged again in the document.

Make the selected   A spelling that
Suggestions change.   shouldn't be altered.

Shows any suggested spellings.

Add the word or usage to the dictionary so that it recognizes the word as correct in the future.

Make the selected **Suggestions** change throughout the worksheet.

Add the spelling error and the correction to the AutoCorrect list to automatically correct in the future.

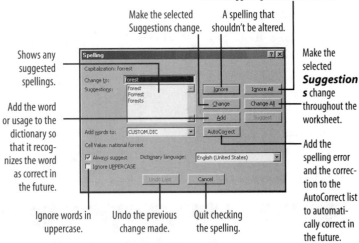

Ignore words in uppercase.

Undo the previous change made.

Quit checking the spelling.

4. Click the [Yes] or [No] button if Excel asks you to continue checking the worksheet, especially if you didn't start checking at the beginning of the worksheet.

5. Click the [OK] button if Excel displays a message telling you the spelling check is complete. This means all inaccuracies have been reviewed.

S T U

TIP

You don't have to be at the beginning of a workbook when you check for spelling errors. If you start in the middle of a workbook, Excel checks until it reaches the end, and then it asks you whether you want to continue checking from the beginning of your workbook.

See Also AutoCorrect, Error Messages

SORT DATA

You can arrange the information in your worksheets by sorting columns alphabetically, numerically, or by date (according to the type of information in your cells).

Sort Data

1. Choose **Data, Sort** to open the Data, Sort to open the Sort dialog box. Excel automatically selects the logical cells in your worksheet or you can pre-select them.

2. Select the **My list has** option depending on whether you have a **Header row** or **No header row**.

3. Click the **Sort by** drop-down list box to select the first column to sort and the corresponding **Ascending** or **Descending** option to establish the sort direction. If you have more than one column by which to sort in a sequence, click one or both of the **Then by** drop-down list boxes and indicate the desired sort direction.

4. Click the [ok] button to accept changes and review the sorted data.

Create a Custom Sort

1. Choose **Tools, Options; Custom Lists** tab to open the Custom Lists dialog box.

2. Select **NEW LIST** from the **Custom lists** drop-down box.

3. Click in the **List entries** drop-down box and enter each list entry in the order that you want the list to be sorted.

4. Click the [Add...] button to add the custom list.

5. Click the [OK] button to return to the worksheet.

6. Choose **Data, Sort** to open the Sort dialog box. Excel automatically selects the logical cells in your worksheet or you can also pre-select them.

7. Click the [Options...] button to open the Sort Options dialog box.

8. Select the **First key sort order** drop-down list, choose the new sort list you just created, and then click the [OK] button.

9. Select any other sort options in the Sort dialog box and click the [OK] button to return to the worksheet.

See Also Data Lists, Filter Data

SPLIT WINDOW

You can simultaneously view two parts of a worksheet if you split the window into multiple panes. This is convenient when you need to view information at different locations in a worksheet, but work in another portion of the worksheet.

Quick Tip	
Feature	*Keyboard Shortcut*
Other Pane	F6 or ⬆Shift+F6

Split the Worksheet View

1. Choose **Window, Split** and click in the worksheet where you want to view the split area. You can click and drag the split bar at any time to adjust the size of each window.

2. Move through each split with the scrollbars to position the worksheet view areas.

3. Double-click a split bar to remove the split, or choose **Window, Remove Split**.

See Also View Multiple Worksheets, Views, Workspace

START EXCEL

When Excel is installed, a copy of the application icon is placed in the Programs menu by default. From this menu, you can launch Excel.

Use the Start Button

1. Click the button in the taskbar to open the Start menu.

2. Click the **Programs** command to open the Programs menu.

3. Click **Microsoft Excel** to start the application.

Create and Use a Shortcut Icon

1. Locate the Excel folder or file (even Excel's executable file .exe) in Windows Explorer.

2. Left-click the folder or file and drag and drop it at the new location, such as your desktop.

3. Select **Create Shortcut(s) Here** from the pop-up menu that appears; the shortcut is created.

S
T
U

4. Double-click the shortcut icon to launch Excel.

See Also Exit Excel, Shortcut Bar, Switch Between Worksheets and Applications

STYLES

Excel contains preset styles that are applied to the cells in your worksheet. The Normal style is the default, but you can apply a different style or create your own.

Quick Tip

Feature	Button	Keyboard Shortcut
Format Style		Alt + ′
Format Cells		Ctrl + 1
General Number Format		Ctrl + ⇧Shift + ~
Currency Format	$	Ctrl + ⇧Shift + $
Percentage Format	%	Ctrl + ⇧Shift + %
Exponential Format		Ctrl + ⇧Shift + ∧
Date Format		Ctrl + ⇧Shift + #
Time Format		Ctrl + ⇧Shift + @
Number Format		Ctrl + ⇧Shift + !

Apply a Cell Style

1. Select the cell(s) that you want to apply a particular style.

2. Choose **Format, Style** to open the Style dialog box.

3. Click the **Style name** drop-down list and select the style you want to apply.

4. Click the ☐OK☐ button to accept your changes and return to the worksheet.

Create a New Style

1. Choose **Format, Style** to open the Style dialog box.

2. Click the **Style name** drop-down list and type in a name for the new style you want to create.

3. Click to select or deselect the **Style includes** options.

4. Click the **Modify** button to open the Format Cells dialog box.

5. Click the **Number, Alignment, Font, Border, Patterns,** and **Protection** tabs and select from the various options to apply the formatting that you want the new style to contain.

6. Click the ☐OK☐ button in both dialog boxes to accept your changes and return to the worksheet.

Copy Styles

1. Open the workbook that contains the styles you want to copy to your current workbook.

2. Choose **Format, Style** to open the Style dialog box.

3. Click the ☐Merge...☐ button to open the Merge Styles dialog box.

4. Select the **Merge styles from** workbook from the list.

5. Click the ☐OK☐ button to accept the styles and return to the workbook.

See Also Fonts, Templates

SUBTOTALS
see Data Lists   pg 38

SUM
see AutoSum   pg 14

SUMIF

The SUMIF function is one of Excel's many built-in formulas for performing a specialized calculation on the data in your worksheet. It totals the cells that meet a set of requirements in a range of data.

Sum Cells If They Meet Criteria

1. Click the cell where you want the result of the function to appear.

2. Click the **Paste Function**  button on the Standard toolbar to open the Paste Function dialog box.

3. Double-click the **SUMIF** option in the **Most Recently Used Function Category, Function Name** list box. Excel automatically inserts what it considers to be the most likely range to be summed, based on the cell that you have chosen for your results.

4. Accept this range or type the cell range or range name you want, press (Tab↹), type the criteria, and then press (↵Enter). The result appears in the active cell and the function is displayed in the Formula bar.

> **TIP**
>
> If Excel doesn't automatically select the cells you want, you can select them yourself by clicking in the first cell, holding down (⇧Shift), and clicking in the last cell.

See Also AVERAGE, COUNTIF, MAX, MIN

SWITCH BETWEEN WORKBOOKS AND APPLICATIONS

You can have multiple Excel workbooks and Office applications open at one time and switch between them whenever you want. Use the Windows taskbar to move quickly from one open application window to another.

Quick Tip	
Feature	*Keyboard Shortcut*
Switch Between Documents and Applications	Alt + Tab⇄

Switch Between Excel and Other Applications

1. Click the Excel button on the Windows taskbar for the workbook you want to use.

2. Click the Windows taskbar button for a different Office application.

See Also Shortcut Bar, Start Excel

TABLES

Excel helps you create data tables based on input values that you define. This can be convenient when you want to show the results of changing values in your table formulas. A one-input data table uses one formula with one list of input values, where a two-input data table uses two lists of input values.

Create a One-Input Data Table

1. Select a range for the data table. The one-input data table is set up as follows:

   ■ Left column—This column contains the values for the single input cell.

- Upper-left cell—This cell is not used in the one-input data table; only the two-input data table.

- Top row—This row contains the formulas or references that calculate formulas in the worksheet.

- Interior remaining cells—These cells contain the results that Excel calculates.

2. Choose **Data, Table** to open the Table dialog box.

3. Select the **Row input cell** if the variables for the input cell are located in a row; select the **Column input cell** if the variables for the input cell are located in a column.

4. Click the ⬜ ᴏᴋ button. Excel uses an array formula that uses the TABLE function, which means the table updates if you change the cell references in the first row or input different values in the first column.

Create a Two-Input Data Table

1. Select a range for the data table. The two-input data table is set up as follows:

- Left column—This column contains the values for the first input cell.

- Upper-left cell—This cell references the single result formula.

- Top row—This row contains the values for the second input cell.

- Interior remaining cells—These cells contain the results that Excel calculates.

2. Choose **Data, Table** to open the Table dialog box.

3. Select the **Row input cell**.

4. Select the **Column input cell**.

5. Click the ⬜ ᴏᴋ button. Excel fills in the table with the results of the calculations.

See Also Data Lists, Goal Seek, PivotTable, Scenarios

TEMPLATES

You can create a workbook template with any type of text, formatting, toolbars, macros, styles, or just about any other setting you can change.

Create and Open a New Workbook Template

1. Click the **New** button on the Standard toolbar to open a new workbook. Type in the data and text, and then format it so that it is how you want the workbook template to appear.
2. Click the **Save** button on the Standard toolbar to open the Save As dialog box.
3. Click the **Save as type** drop-down list box and select **Template**. Any newly created templates will automatically default to the **Templates** folder and have an **.xlt** file extension.
4. Type a filename and click the [Save] button. You can make modifications to this workbook template at any time, just make sure you save the changes.
5. Choose **File**, **Close** to close the workbook.
6. Choose **File**, **New**; **General** tab.
7. Click the workbook template you just created and saved.
8. Click the [OK] button to open the template as a workbook. Now you can work with the workbook and save it as an Excel workbook.

See Also New Worksheet, Save Worksheets, Styles

TEXT
see Fonts   pg 59

TEXT TO COLUMNS

Excel enables you to convert text that you select into a table. If you have data that is listed in text format (delimited or fixed length), you can assign field widths and break the text into columns of data, specifying the data format.

Change Text to Columns

1. Select the text that you want to change into columnar information for a table.

2. Choose **Data, Text to Columns** to open the Convert Text to Columns Wizard.

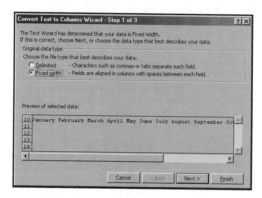

3. Select the **Original data type** of either **Delimited** or **Fixed width** (Excel should automatically default to the most logical choice depending on the selected text). Then, click the `Next >` button.

4. Set the field widths using the following options:

   ■ Create—Click at the desired column position.

   ■ Delete—Double-click on the column line.

   ■ Move—Click and drag the column separators.

   Then, click the `Next >` button.

5. Select the **Column data format** and the **Destination** location of the columnar data. Then, click the `Finish` button to see how your data appears.

TIP

Delimiters can be a tab, semicolon, comma, space, or other types of characters. These are the items that separate one bit of data from another. Qualifiers can have double, single, or no quotes. These are the items that qualify the data as text.

S
T
U

See Also Numbers

TOOLBARS

To perform tasks and access features quickly and easily, you can simply click a toolbar button with your mouse pointer. Doing so is faster than using a menu command, especially for frequent or repetitive tasks. The Standard toolbar contains buttons for the most common commands. The Formatting toolbar contains lists and buttons for the most common formatting commands.

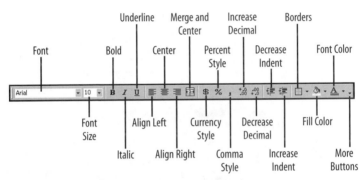

Float and Dock a Toolbar

1. Click the vertical bar on the leftmost side of the toolbar, and drag and drop the toolbar onto your desktop so that it looks like it is floating on top of your desktop.

2. Click on the toolbar title and drag it to a different edge on the desktop so it looks like it is docked.

3. Double-click on the title portion of the toolbar and the toolbar automatically returns to its previous location.

Show and Hide Toolbars

1. Choose **View**, **Toolbars**, and select the toolbar you want to show. Toolbars that are displayed have checks next to their names in the menu.

2. Choose **View**, **Toolbars**, and deselect the toolbar you want to hide. The check mark in the menu and on the toolbar onscreen, disappear.

Add or Remove Buttons

1. Click the **More Buttons** ⬒ button on the toolbar you want to customize and select **Add or Remove Buttons**.

2. Check a particular command button to add it to the toolbar; uncheck a command button to remove it from the toolbar.

Create a New Toolbar

1. Choose **Tools, Customize; Toolbar** tab.

2. Click the [New...] button, type in the name of the new toolbar, and click the [OK] button.

3. Click the **Commands** tab in the Customize dialog box and select a button from the **Categories** and **Commands** list boxes.

4. Click and drag the command to the location you want and drop it on a toolbar.

5. Click the [Close] button on the Customize dialog box.

Modify a New Toolbar Command Button Image

1. Choose **Tools, Customize; Commands** tab.

2. Select the toolbar **Category**.

3. Click the command button on the toolbar you want to modify; it appears with a black line around it.

4. Choose **Modify Selection, Change Button Image**, and select an image.

5. Click the [Modify Selection ▾] button and choose **Default Style**, which displays only the button image.

6. Click the [Close] button on the Customize dialog box.

See Also Menus, Shortcut Bar

TRACK CHANGES

Sometimes you find that you have to make corrections in a worksheet, or perhaps you are working on a report in a team environment. To determine who made which changes when, you can track the changes onscreen with revision marks.

Track Worksheet Changes

1. Choose **Tools, Track Changes, Highlight Changes** to open the Highlight Changes dialog box.

2. Select from the available tracking options.

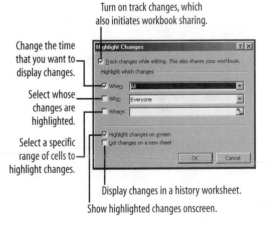

Turn on track changes, which also initiates workbook sharing.

Change the time that you want to display changes.

Select whose changes are highlighted.

Select a specific range of cells to highlight changes.

Display changes in a history worksheet.

Show highlighted changes onscreen.

3. Click the ▭ox▭ button to accept changes and return to the worksheet.

See Also Accept and Reject Changes, Share Workbooks

TROUBLESHOOT
see Detect and Repair   pg 45

UNDERLINE
see Format   pg 61

UNDO AND REDO

Undo and Redo are convenient when you want to see how your worksheet looks with and without changes you make. In addition, this option is convenient when you have made an error in your worksheet. You can undo and redo data changes, formatting options, and more.

Quick Tip

Feature	Button	Keyboard Shortcut
Undo	🔙	Ctrl+Z or Alt+←Backspace
Redo or Repeat	🔜	Ctrl+Y or Alt+⬆Shift+←Backspace or F4 or Alt+↵Enter

Use Undo and Redo

1. Type or make a change(s) in your worksheet.
2. Click the **Undo** 🔙 button as many times as necessary to undo the change(s).
3. Click the **Redo** 🔜 button as many times as necessary to redo the change(s).

> **TIP**
>
> You can also click the **Undo** or **Redo** drop-down list arrows to select the exact changes you want to make. If you select the third change down the list, for example, to be undone, actions one and two will also be undone.

See Also Close Worksheets, Save Worksheets

VALIDATION

see Data Lists   pg 38

VIEW MULTIPLE WORKSHEETS

If you don't want to constantly switch between worksheets, you can view multiple Excel worksheets onscreen. The worksheet displaying a darker title bar is considered the active worksheet; when you type, text goes there.

View Multiple Worksheets

1. Open all the worksheets you want to simultaneously view.

2. Choose **Window, Arrange All**.

3. Click on the title bar or in the body of the worksheet where you want to work.

> **TIP**
>
> To return to viewing only one entire worksheet, double-click the title bar of the worksheet in which you want to work.

See Also Open Worksheets, Split Windows, Workspace

VIEWS

see Workspace   pg 144

WATERMARKS

Images that appear grayed out behind text are called watermarks. An electronic watermark can be made by typing
text over a graphic image.

Create a Watermark

1. Right-click on a graphic that you have inserted or created in your worksheet and choose **Format Picture**
   from the shortcut menu.

2. Click the **Color** drop-down list in the **Image control**
   section and choose **Watermark**.

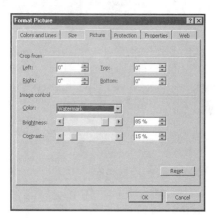

3. Click the [OK] button to accept the changes and
   return to your worksheet.

See Also Clip Art, Print

WEB PAGES

You can view your worksheets as Web pages in Web Page
Preview even before you have saved the file as a Web page.
Once you save a workbook as a Web page, you can load it
to your Web site.

Quick Tip	
Feature	*Keyboard Shortcut*
Web Go Back	[Alt]+[←]
Web Go Forward	[Alt]+[→]

Use Web Page Preview

1. Choose, **File**, **Web Page Preview** to open the Internet Explorer browser and display your worksheet.

2. Click the **Back** ⬅ button to return to the Excel worksheet.

Save As a Web Page

1. Choose **File**, **Save as Web Page** to open the Save As dialog box.

2. Click the **Places bar** option for the location of the file you want to save. Click the **Save in** drop-down list box to help locate the correct folder or drive. You can also click the **Up One Level** ⬆ button to move through folders.

3. Click the **Selection: Sheet** option if you want to save only the current worksheet as a Web page; the **Add interactivity** check box becomes available, click this option if you want to be able to enter and calculate data on the Web.

4. Click the ⬜ Change Title... button and type in a **Page title** if you want the page title to be different than the filename, and click the ⬜ OK button. Note that the ⬜ Publish button allows you to select each of these options in one main Publish as a Web Page dialog box.

5. Type the filename and click the ⬜ Save button.

V
W
X

TIP

Instead of saving the entire default workbook, you can select the option **Selection: Sheet** to save only the active worksheet as a Web page.

See Also Backgrounds, Email, Save Workbooks, Workspace

WHAT-IF ANALYSIS
see Scenarios   pg 121

WORKSHEETS

A new workbook includes three sheets by default. You can easily name, add, delete, and copy worksheets.

Quick Tip

Feature	*Keyboard Shortcut*
Insert New Worksheet	⬆Shift + F11 or Alt + ⬆Shift + F1
Insert Chart Sheet	Alt + F1

Name Worksheets

1. Double-click the sheet tab of the sheet you want to rename; the current name is highlighted.
2. Type the new name and press ↵Enter. Excel displays the new name on the worksheet tab.

Insert a Worksheet

1. Click on a worksheet tab. This will be the worksheet where the new worksheet is added *before* it.
2. Choose **Insert, Worksheet**. Excel inserts a new blank worksheet. This new worksheet is selected.

Delete a Worksheet

1. Click the sheet you want to delete.
2. Choose **Edit, Delete Sheet**.

3. Click the [OK] button to confirm the deletion. The worksheet and all its data is deleted.

> **WARNING**
> You cannot undo the action of deleting a worksheet. Make sure you have a backup copy of the workbook or are positive that you will never need the worksheet again.

Copy a Worksheet to Another Workbook

1. Open the workbooks you want to copy from and copy to. Click the worksheet tab you want to copy.

2. Choose **Edit, Move or Copy Sheet** to open the Move or Copy dialog box.

3. Click the **To Book** drop-down list and select the workbook you want to move it to.

4. Select the tab order location you want to place the copy of the worksheet.

5. Click the **Create a copy** check box.

6. Click the [OK] button; the worksheet is copied.

See Also Open Workbooks, Save Workbooks, Workspace

WORDART

WordArt is a feature that allows you to insert text that looks graphical itself. You can select from different styles of colors and arrangements of lettering.

Add WordArt

1. Click the **Drawing** button on the Standard toolbar to open the Drawing toolbar.

2. Click the **WordArt** button on the Drawing toolbar.

3. Double-click a WordArt style in the WordArt Gallery dialog box and type the text in the Edit WordArt Text dialog box.

4. Click the [OK] button to insert the WordArt and return to your workbook.

Edit WordArt

1. Double-click the WordArt object to edit the text, the font, and/or the font size; click the [OK] button to return to the workbook.

2. Click directly on the WordArt object and drag it to a new location or click the mouse pointer on one of the object handles and drag to resize the WordArt.

See Also, Clip Art, Drawing Tools, Files, Objects

WORKSPACE

You can click the scrollbars to move the view of the worksheet. Press the arrow keys on the keyboard to move the cursor through the worksheet, use the zoom control to see various amounts of the worksheet at once; view/hide the formula bar/status bar, or review a worksheet in full screen.

Quick Tip

Feature	*Button*	*Keyboard Shortcut*
End Row Left		Ctrl + ←
End Row Right		Ctrl + →
End Column Up		Ctrl + ↑
End Column Down		Ctrl + ↓
Minimize Workbook Window	▭	Ctrl + F9
Maximize Workbook Window	▣	Ctrl + F10
Move Workbook Window		Ctrl + F7
Restore Workbook Window	▣	Ctrl + F5
Size Workbook Window		Ctrl + F8

Save Workspace

1. Format the workspace as you want it to appear each time you work in Excel. Each open workbook, size, and position will be stored in a workspace file.

2. Choose **File, Save Workspace** to open the Save Workspace dialog box.

3. Type in a filename and click the [🖫 Save] button. The file is saved in the **Add-Ins** folder.

4. Exit Excel and open the workspace file you just saved; the workbooks you had open appear just as you saved them in the workspace before you exited Excel.

Use Scrollbar Options

1. Click on the scrollbar arrows to scroll through the worksheet. Or, click directly on the scrollbar itself and drag it up and down to quickly move through the worksheet.

2. Click the beginning, previous, next, and end arrows on the left side of the worksheet tabs to move through the worksheets, when there is more data than can be viewed at once.

Increase Worksheet View Size

1. Click the **Zoom** drop-down list on the Standard toolbar.

2. Select the percentage or descriptive size you want to view your worksheet in. You can also click directly on the **Zoom** list box and type in an exact zoom percentage.

Use Page Break Preview

1. Choose **View, Page Break Preview**.

2. Click and drag the page break lines to adjust where your page breaks are set in your print area.

3. Choose **View, Normal** to return to the Normal view.

V
W
X

View Full Screen

Choose **View, Full Screen** to view the worksheet with only the Full Screen toolbar to close the full screen. You can move the mouse pointer to the top of the screen and the menu commands appear.

Alter View Options

1. Choose **Tools, Options; View** tab.

Enables you to view the comments in the worksheet

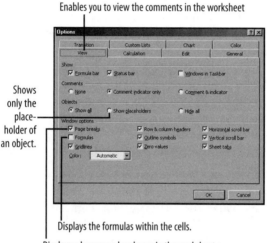

Shows only the place-holder of an object.

Displays the formulas within the cells.

Displays where page breaks are in the worksheet.

2. Click the options that you would like to be able to view in your worksheets at all times.

3. Choose the [OK] button to accept changes and return to the worksheet.

See Also Save Workbooks, Worksheet Map, Views

ZOOM
see Workspace   pg 144

INDEX